HOLDING TOGETHER

EQUALITIES, DIFFERENCE AND COHESION

Guidance for school improvement planning

Robin Richardson

Trentham Books

Stoke on Trent, UK and Sterling, USA

Trentham Books Limited
Westview House   22883 Quicksilver Drive
734 London Road   Sterling
Oakhill   VA 20166-2012
Stoke on Trent   USA
Staffordshire
England ST4 5NP

First published 2009

British Library Cataloguing-in-Publication Data
A catalogue record for this book is available from the British Library

ISBN: 978 1 85856 453 1

Designed and typeset by Trentham Print Design Ltd, Chester and printed in Great Britain by Page Bros (Norwich) Ltd., Norfolk

Contents

ACKNOWLEDGEMENTS

This book was commissioned by Derbyshire County Council's Children and Younger Adults' Department as a follow-up to *Here, There and Everywhere*, published for Derbyshire by Trentham Books in 2004, reprinted 2005. It has a broadly similar format as the earlier book and contains a small amount of the same material. Acknowledgement is due to the headteachers, teachers, advisers and officers, coordinated by Steve Ford, who assisted with both publications. Opinions expressed or implied in the book are the responsibility of the author and do not necessarily represent official policy of Derbyshire County Council.

Acknowledgement is due also to the participants in national conferences on single equality policies organised by the Department for Children, Schools and Families (DCSF) in 2008 and 2009, and to documents produced in a range of local authorities and specialist organisations.

Descriptions of curriculum concepts and processes in Part Three are based on guidance issued by the Qualifications and Curriculum Authority.

INTRODUCTION
HOLDING TOGETHER

Our children can fly

On Wednesday 5 November 2008, and on the following days, a brief piece of verse spread like lightning round the world. It came in text messages and emails, bulletins and newsletters, raps and songs, on blogs and networking sites, T-shirts and greetings cards, phone-ins and chat shows. Rosa Parks sat, it started, so Dr King could walk. Dr King walked, it continued, so Barack could run. Barack ran, the story went on, so he could lead. He is leading now, it concluded, so our children can fly.

A step change in history, it felt, was taking place – and not only in the United States but in the whole world; and not only in the story of race relations and racisms but also in stories about humankind's struggles for equality more generally. In his acceptance speech on 5 November 2008, the new president-elect paid tribute to his whole country: 'young and old, rich and poor, Democrat and Republican, black, white, Hispanic, Asian, Native American, gay, straight, disabled and not disabled'.

The celebrations referred to famous individuals – Rosa Parks, Martin Luther King, Barack Obama. Also they recalled mass movements, mobilisations and marches involving millions on millions of people whose names are known only to their families and networks of friends. The more general story similarly involved not only famous individuals but also vast and countless numbers of others. It contains the struggles for equality between women and men; for the dignity and rights of disabled people; for recognition of and attention to worldviews based on religion; for justice for lesbian women and gay men; for the inclusion of the youngest and oldest members of society, for ending disadvantages around birth, caste, class and poverty.

This book

This book is about holding together the various strands in that larger story, particularly in the field of education. It reflects what teachers are doing throughout the world, in alliance with the young people and children in their schools, and with parents and other carers, to spread information about equalities, difference and togetherness, and inspire the younger generation to play their part. 'How wonderful it is,' reflected Anne Frank in her diary, 'that no one needs to wait a single moment before starting to improve the world'.

Reflections – 1

Can fly
Rosa Parks sat,
so Dr King could walk.

Dr King walked,
so Barack could run.

Barack ran,
so he could lead.

He is leading now,
so our children can fly.

Anon, 5 November 2008, adapted from words by Jay-Z

Strands and subjects

Specifically, this book is about holding together:

- the six strands and areas of human difference in European and British equalities legislation – age, disability, ethnicity, faith, gender, sexuality

- the seventh strand of social class

- the duty that schools have to promote community cohesion

- being a citizen of the world.

In addition, the book is about holding together the subjects of the school curriculum – art, craft and design; citizenship, design and technology; English language and literacy; geography; history; information and communications technology; mathematics; modern foreign languages; music; personal, social, health and economic education; physical education and dance; religious education; science.

The book's title

They are rich, these two words, in echoes, suggestions, hints and associations – '*hold*' and '*together*'.

Hold

Hold back, hold court, hold dear, hold the fort, hold good, hold water, hold your breath, your head high, your ground, your horses, your own, your tongue.

We hold, declared the founding parents of the United States of America, certain truths to be self-evident. The first and foremost of these, they declared, is that all human beings are of equal value.

'The centre cannot hold', lamented a poet near the start of the twentieth century, and in consequence 'mere anarchy is loosed upon the world'. 'Hold infinity', said another poet around 100 years earlier, 'in the palm of your hand, and eternity in an hour'. 'Hold fast,' proclaimed a great religious teacher near the dawn of the first millennium, 'to that which is good'.

The word *hold* is derived from Old English *haldan*, meaning watch over, guard, defend, care for, look after, keep safe. The modern English word *behold* originally meant watch thoroughly, watch closely, watch with wrapt attention.

There is no linguistic connection between the words *hold* and *whole*. It is a happy coincidence, though, that they sound so alike. Holding things together involves working with wholes. The word *whole*, for its part, is connected with *healing* and *health*, and *well*.

Together

Stick together, put two and two together, we're all in this together, get it together, pull yourself together, togetherness, she's a very together person.

'We must hang together', said one of the founding parents of the United States to another, 'or we shall certainly hang separately'. 'All things work together for good', maintained a religious teacher. 'We've been together for forty years,' went an old music hall song. 'The time and the place and the loved one,' dreamed and yearned a poet, 'all together'.

The word *together* is derived from Old English *togadere*, meaning association, company, fellowship, gathering. It is connected with modern English *gather*, with its twin implications of collecting and understanding.

An ancient symbol

The ancient Chinese symbol of *yin* and *yang* is an icon of holding together. Things which appear different from each other are in fact interdependent, claims the symbol, part of a larger whole; and everything is shaped, it claims further, by its apparent opposite yet everything also contains its own opposite. In the colour scheme on the cover of this book, for example, the yellow shape is moulded by the purple shape, and the purple by the yellow, within the encompassing oval. At the same time the yellow contains some purple and the purple contains some yellow. Neither shape is entirely separate from the other. Life is a matter of both/and, not either/or.

The *yin* and *yang* icon can be applied to light/dark, gentleness/strength, activity/repose, controlling/letting go, receiving/giving, work/play, self/other, you/me, us/them. It can be applied also to equalities legislation. Each strand in the legislation is a spectrum or continuum on which there are many points – the strands do not consist of binary opposites. This is most obvious in the case of age. It is true also, however, though less obviously, in the case of all the other strands as well. 'I note the obvious differences between each sort and type,' wrote Maya Angelou in her poem *The Human Family*, 'but we are more alike, my friends, than we are unalike'.

Background

This book has its origins in the education system of one country, England, and in one particular local authority, Derbyshire. It is relevant in other parts of the United Kingdom as well, however. It reflects educational projects and developments not only in the UK but also, amongst others, in Australia, Ireland, South Africa and the United States.

It is a sequel to *Here, There and Everywhere*, compiled in Derbyshire in 2004. The main differences between the earlier book and this are as follows:

- The earlier book focused primarily on ethnicity and 'race', whereas this is concerned with all the strands in equalities legislation.

- This book is also concerned with class, cohesion and rights, and with education for global citizenship.

- The earlier book reflected the national curriculum that was in operation in England at the time. This version takes into account developments that have taken place since then.

At the time of writing (early 2009) it is expected that a new Equality Bill will soon be published in Britain and that its requirements will include a positive duty on all public bodies to promote greater equality in relation to age, disability, ethnicity, faith, gender, sexuality and transgender. This book reflects the spirit of the legislation that is expected, but not the exact letter.

Reflections – 3

Love the questions themselves

We must not refuse to become aware of all that we find distressing or painful or fearful within. If we do, we shall merely project onto others our own inner darkness.

Are you white and afraid of your blackness?

Are you male and afraid of the feminine within?

Are you heterosexual and afraid of your homosexual feelings? Are you rich and afraid of your poverty?

Are you young and afraid of being old?

Are you healthy and afraid of your mortality?

Are you able and afraid of disability?

Are you busily involved and afraid of being useless?

Nothing is to be expelled as foreign.

All is to be befriended and transformed.

Be patient towards all that is unsolved in your heart.

Try to love the questions themselves.

– Jim Cotter, 1988, drawing partly on Letters to a Young Poet *by Rainer Maria Rilke, written in the period 1903-08*

hold *v.* **1.** have, keep, maintain, occupy, own, possess, retain **2.** adhere, clasp, cleave, clinch, cling, clutch, cradle, embrace, enfold, grasp, grip, stick **3.** arrest, check, curb, detain, restrain, stop **4.** assume, believe, consider, deem, entertain, judge, maintain, presume, reckon, regard, think, view **5.** continue, endure, last, persevere, persist, remain, remain, stay **6.** assemble, conduct, convene, run **7.** bear, carry, shoulder, support **8.** accommodate, have a capacity for **9.** apply, be in force, be the case, operate, remain valid, stand up

together *adv.* **1.** as a group, as one, closely, collectively, hand in glove, in a body, in concert, in cooperation, jointly, side by side **2.** all at once, at the same time, concurrently, with one accord **3.** continuously, one after another, without a break, without interruption **4.** arranged, fixed, ordered, organised, settled, sorted out – *adj.* **5.** calm, composed, cool, stable, well-adjusted, well-balanced, well-organised

Summary of contents

As shown in the table of contents on an earlier page, the book has four sections after this introduction.

First there are briefing notes on nine strands or areas of human difference and similarity. Each strand is covered in much the same way: there are reminders of the legal and ethical context; points about key ideas and distinctions; some reflections from novels, poetry, drama and journalism; and reminders of key challenges and priorities for schools.

Second there are notes on points arising. These are to do with principles underlying legislation, terminology and semantics, prejudice-related bullying and incidents, big ideas across the curriculum and at all ages, and issues of practical pedagogy and classroom methodology.

Third, there are notes on the 14 subjects or skills in the English secondary curriculum. They reflect changes currently (early 2009) being considered in relation to the primary curriculum. Each subject is covered here in much the same way: commentary on the importance of the subject in relation to the nine strands of equality discussed earlier; some evocative quotations; and some possible classroom activities.

Fourth, there are notes on the historical background; on the legislative frameworks currently in operation in the UK; points for a school's action plan in relation to equalities; and a substantial list of websites.

Reflections

Throughout the book there are boxes which are set apart from the main text. They have the generic title 'Reflections'. Each contains a quotation (or occasionally two or more quotations), mostly from novels, poetry, drama and journalism. The overall purpose is to illustrate the main text by evoking emotional and intellectual issues which invite or require further thought. The quotations are talking points, not statements to be agreed with. Most are serious but a handful are humorous or light-hearted.

Here is an extremely brief selection of them, to show what is in store.

Proud

I am a Glaswegian Pakistani teenage woman of Muslim descent, who supports Glasgow Rangers in a Catholic school, 'cause I'm a mixture and I'm proud of it.
(*Character in a film by Ken Loach*)

Not also fight

I could not have fought against the discrimination of apartheid and not also fight against the discrimination that homosexuals endure, even in our churches and faith groups.'
(*Archbishop Desmond Tutu*)

Freely and supple

May my mind walk about freely and supple
and even if it's Sunday may I be wrong
for whenever men are right they are no longer
young. (*e.e. cummings*)

Nasty words

People used to call children like the children at school spaz and crip and mong, which were nasty words ... Sometimes the children from the school down the road see us in the street when we are getting off the bus and they shout, 'Special Needs! Special Needs!'
(*Novel by Mark Haddon*)

Concluding note

This book began by recalling the high hopes and expectations that swept through the world's education systems, and through the world more generally, in November 2008. During the book's shelf-life there will no doubt be setbacks and disappointments and the earlier optimism may seem a dream. The book has been compiled and designed, however, with the intention of keeping the equalities agenda in education alive, and of sustaining confidence in it, even at the most difficult times. Overleaf, there is a visual summary of the nine-point agenda as a whole. The agenda is necessarily about large-P and small-p politics. The visual summary, though, has an individual human being at its core. In the following chapter, there are nine sets of preliminary briefing notes.

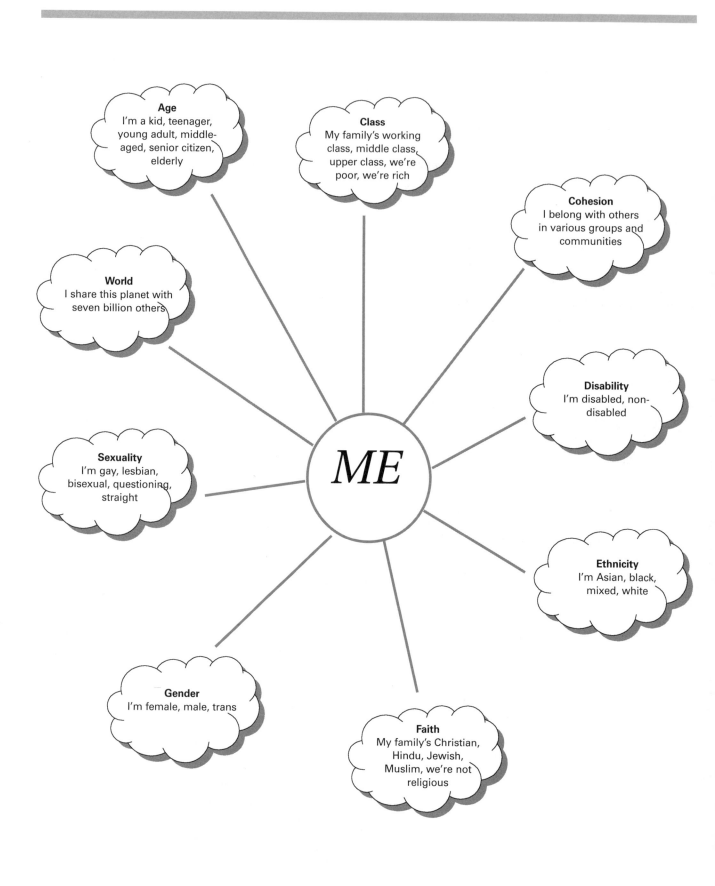

Part One
Strands and challenges: briefing notes

This section of the book contains briefing notes on nine strands or areas of human difference and similarity.

In relation to each strand you will find here:

■ reminders of the legal and ethical context

■ points about key terms and distinctions

■ reflections from novels, poetry and journalism

■ reminders of key challenges and priorities for schools.

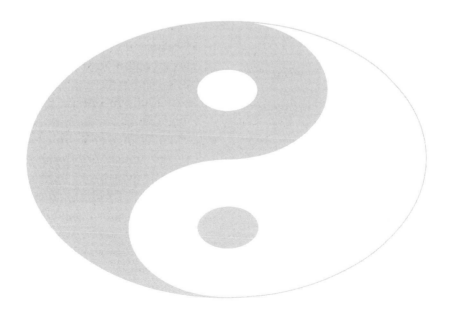

Age

Legal and ethical background

As employers, schools and other educational settings may not discriminate on grounds of age in relation to staff under 65. In the provision of education to young people, however, it is lawful, as also usually essential, to take into account differences of age – though without forgetting, of course, that children and young people have rights under the Convention on the Rights of the Child.

The ethical principle underlying the law is that older people should be valued by society, not ignored, marginalised or excluded. Also, the experiences and outlooks of young people should be valued. This often needs affirming in schools, since in the media negative portrayals of young people are widespread. Generally, there needs to be greater mutual respect, knowledge and understanding between younger people and older.

In addition to law and ethical principles, there are sound pragmatic reasons for ending discrimination against older people. Their contributions to the economy are needed and people in paid employment have better physical and mental health and higher levels of wellbeing and satisfaction with their lives than those who are retired or unemployed. Proportionately, older people are more likely than others to take part in local politics and affairs, and to be involved in the management committees of charities and in the governing bodies of schools. Frequently they are key contributors to the cohesive forces that bind communities together.

Terms and distinctions

The term *ageism* was coined in the United States by Dr Robert Neil Butler towards the end of the 1960s. Butler had himself been brought up by his grandparents and had frequently been shocked by the ways in which his friends and peers talked and thought about people who were the same age as his grandparents. His best known work is *Why Survive? – being old in America* (1975). He maintained that ageism, in common with racism and sexism, has three components, to do respectively with attitudes, behaviour and contexts. (For further discussion, see 'The ABC of prejudice, discrimination and exclusion (page 25). In the case of ageism, the three components are:

Reflections – 4

It strikes me as unjust

Cody, listen. I was special too once, to someone. I could just reach out and lay a fingertip on his arm while he was talking and instantly he would fall silent and get all confused. I had hopes, I was courted, I had the most wonderful wedding. I had three lovely pregnancies, where every morning I would wake up knowing something wonderful would happen in nine months, eight months, seven ... so it seemed I was full of light, it was light and plans that filled me. And then while you children were little, why, I was the center of your worlds! I was everything to you! It was Mother this and Mother that, and Where's Mother? Where's she gone to? And the moment you came in from school, 'Mother? Are you home?' It's not fair, Cody. It's really not fair; now I'm old and I walk along unnoticed, just like anyone else. It strikes me as unjust, Cody. But don't tell the others I said so.

– *from* Dinner at the Homesick Restaurant *by Anne Taylor, 1992*

- negative and dismissive attitudes towards older people

- discriminatory behaviour which involves older people being treated less favourably than younger

- institutional contexts in which negative attitudes and discriminatory behaviour are the norm, and where older people are not listened to.

More recently, the term *ageism* has been applied to the demonisation of children and young people in the media, and in the mindsets and conversations of many adults. In autumn 2008, a YouGov poll in Britain found that half of the 2,021 adults interviewed felt children should be regarded as 'dangerous'; about 54 per cent thought British children behave like 'animals'; more than a third agreed that the streets were 'infested' with children; and about 49 per cent said they disagreed with the statement that children who 'get into trouble' were 'misunderstood' and needed professional help. It was also in autumn 2008 that the United Nations claimed there was a 'general climate of intolerance' towards children in Britain and this could result in them being treated unfairly.

Figure 1: The mental sketch map with which younger people may see older

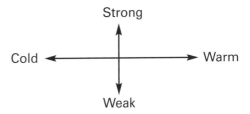

Going round anti-clockwise from the top left, older people may be perceived as hostile and competent – grumpy and interfering; or else (bottom left) cold and weak – moaning and complaining; or else (bottom right) warm and weak – or 'dear and doddery'; or (top right) as warm and strong – having wisdom and dignity, and good will towards the young. Older people have a similar range of views of the young.

Reflections – 5

Very horrible, aren't they?

Until I grew up I thought I hated everybody. But when I grew up I realised it was just children I didn't like. Once you started meeting grown-ups life was much pleasanter. Children are very horrible, aren't they? Selfish, noisy, cruel, vulgar little brutes.

– Philip Larkin, 1960s

Research at the University of Kent, published by Age Concern in 2006, found that attitudes towards older people could be measured along two separate dimensions – strong/weak and cold/warm. The dimensions of cold/warm and strong/weak can be visualised as providing the four poles in mental maps, as depicted in Figure 1.

Reflections – 7

Freely and supple

May my mind walk about freely and supple
and even if it's Sunday may I be wrong
for whenever men are right they are no longer young.

– e.e. cummings (1892-1964)

Reflections – 6

See ME

What do you see, nurses, what do you see?
Are you thinking, when you look at me —
A crabby old woman, not very wise,
Uncertain of habit, with far-away eyes,
Who dribbles her food and makes no reply,
When you say in a loud voice –
'I do wish you'd try.'

...

I'm an old woman now and nature is cruel —
'Tis her jest to make old age look like a fool.
The body is crumbled, grace and vigour depart,
There is now a stone where once was a heart,
But inside this old carcass a young girl still dwells,
And now and again my battered heart swells.

I remember the joys, I remember the pain,
And I'm loving and living life over again,
I think of the years, all too few — gone too fast,
And accept the stark fact that nothing can last -
So open your eyes, nurses, open and see,
Not a crabby old woman, look closer, nurses
– see ME!

Said to have been found in the belongings of an elderly woman after she died in hospital. 1960s

---

Age Equality: challenges for schools

Encouraging and promoting positive attitudes towards older people amongst pupils

Teaching about ageism as a serious form of prejudice and discrimination in modern societies.

Involving older people in the public life of the school.

Challenging hostile prejudices towards children and young people in the media and the general population.

Giving a voice to children and young people of all ages.

Class

Legal and ethical context

The concept of class does not feature in European anti-discrimination legislation. However, social origin is explicitly referred to in the European Convention on Human Rights (ECHR), incorporated into UK law in 1998, and it appears also in the Universal Declaration of Human Rights, 1948. The key words in the ECHR are as follows: 'The enjoyment of the rights and freedoms set forth in this Convention shall be secured without discrimination on any ground such as sex, race, colour, language, religion, political or other opinion, national or *social origin*, association with a national minority, property, *birth* or other status' (Italics added).

There is also recognition internationally that descent-based inequalities (including those that are caste-based) are a serious injustice in many countries and that legal measures should be taken against them.

All mainstream political parties in Britain declare that reducing inequalities based on birth and social origin is major policy aim. In 2008 a Cabinet Office paper entitled *Realising Britain's Potential* noted that 'there remain persistent gaps between the life chances of people from different backgrounds starting from birth and continuing throughout their lives. This is a key future challenge for Britain.' The Children's Plan has two linked objectives: tackling disadvantage experienced by children now, and promoting social mobility in the longer term.

Inequalities relating to disability, ethnicity and gender cannot be adequately addressed unless there is attention also to the ways in which they intertwine with inequalities related to class.

Terms and distinctions

There are differences amongst human beings in relation to wealth, income, occupation, status, prestige, educational qualifications and influence. Related to these there are differences in housing, health levels, lifespan, leisure activities, consumption patterns, aspirations and life chances. The term 'class' is a shorthand way of pointing towards these differences.

There is no standard definition of social class and no standard way of deciding which class someone belongs to. There is general agreement, however, that

---

Reflections – 8

Two nations

'Well, society may be in its infancy,' said Egremont slightly smiling, 'but say what you like, our Queen reigns over the greatest nation that ever existed.'

'Which nation?' asked the younger stranger, 'for she reigns over two.'

The stranger paused. Egremont was silent, but looked inquiringly.

'Yes,' resumed the stranger after a moment's interval. 'Two nations, between whom there is no intercourse and no sympathy, who are as ignorant of each other's habits, thoughts and feelings, as if they were dwellers in different zones or inhabitants of different planets; who are formed by a different breeding, are fed by different food, are ordered by different manners, and are not governed by the same laws.'

'You speak of -?' said Egremont hesitatingly.

'The rich and the poor.'

– *from* Sybil *by Benjamin Disraeli, 1845*

---

it is not helpful for policy-making, though it may be for a novelist wishing to make a point as vividly as possible (see the quotation above from Disraeli's novel *Sybil*), to divide everyone into two categories, simply based on the amount of their wealth. Similarly in the modern educational system, incidentally, it is generally not helpful to divide all pupils into only two groups, those who are entitled to free school meals and those who are not.

The eightfold classification of social class used by the Labour Force Survey (LFS) focuses on occupation:

- higher managerial and professional (about 11 per cent of the UK population)
- lower managerial and professional (22)
- intermediate occupations (10)
- small employers and own account workers (8)
- lower supervisory and technical (9)
- semi-routine occupations (13)
- routine occupations (9)
- never worked or unemployed, or not elsewhere classified (19).

The ACORN system (a classification of residential neighbourhoods) is based on the postcodes where people live and involves distinguishing five broad categories of postcode, named in shorthand as 'wealthy achievers', 'urban prosperous', ' comfortably off', 'moderate means' and 'hard pressed'. Each of these main categories is divided into several sub-categories. The relationship between a pupil's postcode and their educational achievement, measured as obtaining five good passes at GCSE including English and maths, is shown in Table 1.

Table 1: Attainment of pupils at 16+ in England in 2007, according to the ACORN category of their postcode

ACORN category	All England – % achieving 5 good passes including English and maths
'Wealthy achievers'	65.1
'Urban prosperous'	49.2
'Comfortably off'	50.0
'Moderate means'	36.3
'Hard pressed'	25.7

Source: derived from figures published by the Department for Children, Schools and Families, July 2008

Table 1 strikingly shows that there is a connection between the kind of postcode a pupil lives in and the kind of results they achieve when they take GCSE exams at the age of 16. Two thirds of those who live in 'wealthy achiever' postcodes achieve five good passes at 16+, including English and maths, but in 'hard pressed' areas only a quarter do. There is a similar gap of 40 percentage points in most individual authorities and regions.

The purpose of linking educational achievement and economic circumstances is to get key issues into perspective and to identify more accurately what schools can and cannot do in the short term to raise achievement. The purpose is not – absolutely not – to find excuses for not trying to raise achievement, or for having low expectations of certain pupils.

It is usual to distinguish between absolute poverty and relative. Absolute poverty is when basic human needs are not met. 'What people want and need,' the UK's Department for International Development remarked in *Making Governance Work for the Poor* (2005), 'is enough food to eat and water to drink. A roof over their heads, a job, a school for their children, and medicine and care when they are sick. The chance to live in peace, without fear of violence or war.' In the countries of the Global North basic needs such as these are met – there is little or no absolute poverty. However, relative income and comparative social standing are also significant for people's well-being. For this reason, inequalities of class have to be considered at the same time as inequalities of age, disability, ethnicity, faith, gender and sexuality.

Class Inequality: challenges for schools

Planning and implementing programmes which will close the gaps in achievement between pupils of different social backgrounds and increase the participation of people from lower socio-economic backgrounds in higher and further education.

Fostering and developing the qualities, skills and insights of allies – people who are not themselves affected by poverty or unequal status but who through their actions and advocacy give moral, political and practical support to people who are.

Involving pupils of all backgrounds in the public life of the school.

Creating and regularly reviewing plans for creating greater equality of outcome amongst pupils of different social backgrounds, and reporting on progress to governing bodies.

Cohesion

Legal and ethical context

Schools in England and Wales have a duty to promote community cohesion. It complements the duties in the Race Relations Amendment Act 2000 and the four objectives are a) to close attainment and achievement gaps b) to develop common values of citizenship based on dialogue, mutual respect and acceptance of diversity c) to contribute to building good community relations and challenge all types of discrimination and inequality, and d) to remove barriers to access, participation, progression, attainment and achievement.

The duty is clearly relevant to other strands of equality as well, although this is not explicitly stated. Common values of shared citizenship, for example, apply to issues of disability, gender and sexuality, not only to issues of ethnicity. The duty is related also to the national curriculum requirement that pupils should develop a shared sense of Britishness.

Terms and distinctions

The concept of cohesion was introduced into debates about equality by the Commission on the Future of Multi-Ethnic Britain in 2000. 'Every society,' the commission pointed out, 'needs to be cohesive as well as respectful of diversity, and must find ways of nurturing diversity while fostering a common sense of belonging and a shared identity.'

A society is cohesive, said the commission, if:

- its members have a common commitment to the wellbeing of the community and are related to each other in a way that they are not related to outsiders

- its members are able to find their way around in it, that is, they know how to navigate their way through their society, if they understand its conceptual and cultural grammar, and know how to relate to each other

- its members share a climate of mutual trust, and know that if they make sacrifices today for the wider community, it will take care of them when the need arises.

Subsequently, the concept of cohesion was used by reports into disturbances in northern towns and cities in England in 2001. The reports led in due course to

> **Reflections – 10**
>
> **A messy place**
> The thing I like most about Britishness is its messiness and incompleteness. I am a good example of it myself: I was born in Belfast, brought up in London and educated in Edinburgh. I like the unfinishedness of the idea of Britishness and I think that's what is shaping about it... I hope we will always be a messy, pluralistic place.
>
> *(Michael Boyd, artistic director of the Royal Shakespeare Company, quoted in* The Observer, *2005)*

the legal requirement that all schools should promote community cohesion.

Cohesion as a value has the same importance as equality and respect for difference. The relationship between the three can be visualised as a Venn diagram with three overlapping circles, as in the figure below:

Figure 2: The interconnections of equality, difference and cohesion

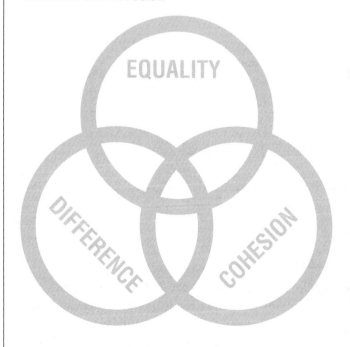

Reflections – 11

The features of a cohesive community

Being a somebody
A community gives its members a sense of belonging, and therefore of their identity and dignity. Here in my community I am among my own people, I am at home, I know them and understand them, and they know and understand me. We speak the same language (including the same body language), smile or laugh at the same jokes, know the same stories and music, have shared memories. I am recognised and respected, I feel that I am a somebody, not a nonentity.

Being looked after
The members of a community take an interest in each other and have a sense of responsibility towards each other. They are prepared to pay taxes or subscriptions for the common good, or to help less fortunate members, and to donate their time to maintaining the community, whether formally or informally. I feel that I will be looked after if I fall on bad times, and that – for example – my children or my elderly and sick parents will be looked after if they get lost.

Feeling grateful
The members of a community are grateful to it, in so far as it does give them a sense of belonging, identity and dignity. My gratitude may take the form of great affection and love, even self-sacrifice, but may also be expressed through criticism and questioning. Sometimes gratitude is expressed more by caring criticism than by blind devotion.

Family quarrels
Communities are not marked by cosiness alone. There are often arguments, quarrels, and profound disagreements. Jockeyings for power and prestige, internal politics, alliances, betrayals. Expulsion or secession is frequently an option. But essentially quarrels within a community are family quarrels. I have a commitment to staying. I cherish the community, and am prepared to compromise in order that the community itself may be maintained.

A range of belongings
Boundaries round a community can be quite hard and fast, making it difficult to join or leave voluntarily. But often they are fluid, unfixed. It is in any case entirely possible for someone to be a significant member of several different communities at the same time; indeed, this is usual. I have, and nearly all people have, a range of belongings, identities and loyalties, and sometimes these are out of tune with each other, or are in blatant conflict.

Symbols and stories
A community is held together by symbols and ceremonies which mean the same to all its members. All the following can have symbolic, not just functional, power, and can help bind a community together symbolically: food; buildings and monuments; rites of passage relating to birth, adolescence, marriage and death; clothes (including uniforms and insignia); religious worship; music – particularly, perhaps, singing; various courtesies, customs, manners and rules of procedure; ritualised conflict in sport and games of all kinds; and – by no means least – iconic stories and narratives, both grand and ordinary. I belong through symbols.

– adapted slightly from The Future of Multi-Ethnic Britain, *2000.*

The features of a cohesive community, summarised above, are applicable at a range of levels: a school or local neighbourhood as well as to society as a whole.

Challenges for schools in relation to community cohesion are listed on page 20.

Disability

Legal and ethical context

It is unlawful in the UK to discriminate on the grounds of disability in employment and the provision of services. The key legislation is the Disability Discrimination Act 1995, as amended by the Disability Discrimination Act 2005. There is further information on pages 86. Legislation in other countries includes the Americans with Disabilities Act (ADA) 1990, modelled on the Civil Rights Act of 1964 which made discrimination based on race, religion, sex and national origin unlawful.

More widely, the Convention on the Rights of Persons with Disabilities was adopted by the United Nations General Assembly in December 2006 and entered into force on 3 May 2008. As of 30 December 2008 there were137 signatories to the Convention, 81 signatories to the Optional Protocol and 44 ratifications.

Reflections – 12

The sense of rejection was enormous

After being turned down by employment agencies, not asked for interviews, sent to the Disablement Resettlement Officer and directed towards some kind of industrial rehabilitation scheme at the day centre that specialised in arts and crafts, I was in a state of shock. I realised that the world of work was even more rigid and inhuman than the education system, which had also excluded me... I was considered unemployable. Unemployable. Unnecessary. Superfluous to need ... The sense of rejection was enormous.

I began to think that no one has the right to decide who should work and who shouldn't. To be able to share our personal gifts, talents, skills, thoughts, care – even love – for the benefit of others is a rational human need. It makes life meaningful. But I also began to realise, slowly, that there is a big difference between having a job in the capitalist sense, i.e. being productive within the economic system for the purposes of the owners, and real work, for the benefit of other human beings.

– from an article by Micheline Mason, 2006

Terms and distinctions

Thinking about disability has developed through three main stages. For much of human history (stage one) the thinking was *pre-scientific*. People with disabilities were seen as possessed by demonic spirits, or perhaps to have received punishment for sins committed in a previous life. They were viewed with fear and disgust and were frequently ostracised and left to beg in order to stay alive. This thinking is reflected nowadays in the harassment and bullying of disabled people in everyday life, including in schools. Such thinking was cruelly present in the European Holocaust of the 1930s and 1940s.

In due course the pre-scientific model was replaced with the *medical model*, which saw disabled people as diseased, deficient or defective and in need of medical attention. The medical model is now challenged by what is known as the *social model*.

In contrast to the medical model, the social model focuses on society and on the barriers that prevent disabled people from participating fully in everyday activities. It sees environmental and cultural factors as the primary cause of disabled people's marginalisation, not their impairment. Barriers are created through fear, ignorance and prejudice, and it is these that cause people to be disabled. It is sometimes suggested that the term 'disablement' should be more widely used in order to stress this. The fundamental aim underlying the social model is to enable and empower disabled people to participate fully and equally in wider society.

A further key distinction in recent thinking is between *impairment* and *disability*. Impairment is a long-term

---

Reflections – 13

This different thinking

We believe that the stress on the social model is helping people in schools and other places where children live and learn to think differently about disability, and what needs to be done to promote equality. And we also believe that this different thinking is having an impact on other areas of equality, like gender and ethnicity.

Department for Children, School and Families, 2008

DISABILITY EQUALITY: THE MEDICAL AND SOCIAL MODELS COMPARED

Core questions	The medical model	The social model
What is the problem?	People with impairments are the problem	Society's customs, practices and attitudes are the problem
Who decides what should be done?	Doctors, psychologists, therapists	Disabled people are involved too -'nothing about us without us'
What should be done?	Separation, segregation, special provision	Inclusion and participation in mainstream institutions and society
What are the motivating emotions?	Pity, sympathy	Respect for dignity and rights
What are the recurring words?	Diagnosis, treatment, cure, able-bodied, normal	Empowerment, human rights, participation
What happens?	Society remains unchanged	Society develops and evolves, and all people benefit

Source: adapted from Disability Equality in Education (DISEED)

characteristic of an individual which affects functioning or appearance, and which may give rise to pain, fatigue, mobility and communication difficulties, and therefore substantially limits a major life activity. Disability is a disadvantage which is caused by barriers, attitudinal as well as physical, that have negative impacts on people with impairments.

Disability Equality: challenges for schools

■ **Equality of outcome**
Planning and implementing programmes which will close the gaps in achievement between disabled and non-disabled children and young people, and increase the participation of disabled young people in higher and further education.

■ **Information base**
Maintaining data on disabilities and impairments which staff and pupils have disclosed and special educational needs which have been identified.

■ **Visibility in the curriculum**
Including disability equality issues and positive images of disabled people in curriculum materials, modules and topics, wherever possible and appropriate.

■ **Understanding**
Ensuring all members of the school community understand the difference between 'the medical model of disability' and 'the social model'.

■ **Preventing and addressing bullying**
Using a range of measures to reduce and remove harassment and bullying of disabled pupils, and promoting positive attitudes towards disabled people.

■ **Involvement**
Ensuring that disabled people are involved in the design and implementation of measures and projects intended to be of benefit to them – 'nothing about us without us' – and listening to their views and voices.

■ **Allies**
Fostering and developing the qualities, skills, insights of allies – people who are not themselves disabled but who through their actions and advocacy give moral, political and practical support to disabled people.

■ **The public life of the school**
Involving disabled pupils in the public life of the school.

■ **Monitoring and review**
Collecting and using a range of quantitative and qualitative evidence to show the extent and nature of progress towards greater disability equality.

■ **Action plans**
Creating and regularly reviewing plans for creating greater disability equality, and reporting on progress to governing bodies.

Ethnicity

Legal and ethical context

It is unlawful to discriminate on grounds of ethnicity in employment and provision of services. The first laws in the UK were enacted in the 1960s but these had little effect. The principal legislation is the Race Relations Act 1976 and the Race Relations (Amendment A) Act 2000. There are details about the general and specific duties on pages 86-7.

Internationally, key legislation includes the International Convention on the Elimination of All Forms of Racial Discrimination (CERD). It was adopted and opened for signature and ratification on 21 December 1965 and entered into force in January 1969. By 2004 it had been ratified by more than 170 countries.

Reflections – 14

Inferior

I went through school with an uneasy suspicion that I was inferior. It may have been a product of the notion that the history of the non-white population of this world is embedded in slavery and colonisation, or perhaps the echoing resonance of the word Paki as it accompanied me through the hostile corridors of the science block.

– Nitin Sawhney, 2004

Terms and distinctions

CERD (see above) defines racial discrimination as 'any distinction, exclusion, restriction or preference based on race, colour, descent, or national or ethnic origin which has the purpose or effect of nullifying or impairing the recognition, enjoyment or exercise, on an equal footing, of human rights and fundamental freedoms in the political, economic, social, cultural or any other field of public life'.

There is a single human race. Terms such as racial group, racial discrimination and race relations are therefore always in danger of being misleading, particularly when they are enshrined in legislation. The term race does, however, invaluably allude to racism. The United Nations World Conference Against Racism (WCAR) in 2001 summarised its concerns with the phrase 'racism, racial discrimination, xenophobia and related intolerance'. The equivalent phrase used by the Council of Europe is 'racism, xenophobia, antisemitism and intolerance'. The definition of racism used by the European Commission against Racism and Intolerance (ECRI) is: '... the belief that a ground such as 'race', colour, language, religion, nationality or national or ethnic origin justifies contempt for a person or a group of persons, or the notion of superiority of a person or group of persons.'

ECRI's references to religion, language and nationality are a reminder that in nearly every kind of racism there is both a biological and a cultural strand. The strands appear in different combinations at different times, however, and in different places. The biological one uses physical features of perceived difference, particularly skin colour and facial features, to recognise 'the other'. The cultural strand refers to differences of religion, language and way of life.

Both strands involve believing that certain differences amongst human beings are fixed as well as significant, that they can justify unjust distributions of power and resources, and can determine who is a full or real member of the national society and who is not. The distinction is sometimes said to be between colour racism and cultural racism, or between North-South racism and West-East racism. Such phrases have their uses, but obscure the reality that physical and cultural markers are usually combined.

Reflections – 15

White outlook

I always found race difficult to understand. It was never intuitive. And the reason was simple. Like every other white person, I had never experienced it myself: the meaning of colour was something I had to learn. The turning point was falling in love with my wife, an Indian-Malaysian, and her coming to live in England. Then, over time, I came to see my own country in a completely different way, through her eyes, her background. Colour is something white people never have to think about because for them it is never a handicap, never a source of prejudice or discrimination, but rather the opposite, a source of privilege. However liberal and enlightened I tried to be, I still had a white outlook on the world.

– Martin Jacques, 2003

The plural term 'racisms' is sometimes used to highlight such complexity. For anti-black racism is different, in terms of its historical and economic origins, and in its contemporary manifestations, stereotypes and effects, from anti-Asian racism. Both are different from, to cite three further significant examples, anti-Irish, anti-Gypsy and anti-Jewish racism. European societies, it is sometimes said, are multi-racist societies.

Specific words have been coined over the years for certain types of racism directed at particular groups – the term antisemitism originated in the mid-nineteenth century, and more recently the terms orientalism and Islamophobia have been coined to refer to anti-Asian racism in general and anti-Muslim racism in particular. Latterly, there has emerged in western Europe a set of phenomena known as anti-refugee racism or xenoracism.

Xenoracism is directed migrant workers and refugees, and people seeking asylum. It gets its energy and support from the millions of white Europeans who are displaced and dispossessed by global forces over which they and their governments have no control. Their employment prospects are threatened and so is the sense of cultural and national identity with which they grew up.

> *Reflections – 16*
> **You can't look**
> The teachers are mostly white. You can't look at a white person and tell if they are a racist, so if they haven't told you their views you can't go to a white person and complain about white racism.
>
> *– student at a school in London, 2004*

Ethnicity Equality: challenges for schools

■ **Equality of outcome**
Planning and implementing programmes which will close the gaps in achievement between pupils of different ethnic, cultural and religious backgrounds and increase the participation of people from minority backgrounds in higher and further education.

■ **Information base**
Maintaining data about the ethnic, religious and cultural backgrounds of staff and pupils.

■ **Visibility in the curriculum**
Including ethnicity equality issues and positive images of people from minority backgrounds in curriculum materials, modules and topics, wherever possible and appropriate.

■ **Preventing and addressing bullying**
Using a range of measures to reduce and remove racist harassment and bullying, and promoting positive attitudes and relationships between pupils of different backgrounds...

■ **Involvement**
Ensuring that people of minority backgrounds are involved in the design and implementation of measures and projects intended to be of benefit to them – 'nothing about us without us' – and listening to their views and voices.

■ **Allies**
Fostering and developing the qualities, skills, insights and allies – people who are not themselves targeted by racism but who through their actions and advocacy give moral, political and practical support to people who are.

■ **The public life of the school**
Involving pupils of all backgrounds in the public life of the school.

■ **Monitoring and review**
Collecting and using a range of quantitative and qualitative evidence to show the extent and nature of progress towards greater ethnicity equality.

■ **Action plans**
Creating and regularly reviewing plans for creating greater ethnicity equality, and reporting on progress to governing bodies.

Faith

Legal and ethical context

There is a legal duty to avoid discrimination on grounds of religion or belief both in employment and in the delivery of services. There are fuller details on page 88. On the other side of the same legislative coin, there is a duty to make reasonable adjustments to accommodate the wishes, preferences and values of employees and service users related to their religious affiliation or faith.

The law does not attempt to lay down what exactly is reasonable, nor with precision what is or is not to count as a religious value or preference. Preliminary guidance has been provided by the Department for Trade and Industry, however, and case law is evolving. It will be complemented by negotiation and reflection in each separate institution.

Reflections – 17

Unable to accept our differences

In his song *Imagine*, John Lennon urged us to dream of a world free from religious faith. I hate to disagree with a Beatle, but that is bad advice. It is easy to pluck incendiary quotations from a holy book and say, 'Look: here is proof — religion is all about revenge and war.' Nor is it hard to catalogue the crimes committed in God's name and so blame religion for all our troubles. But that is like saying that because of floods, the world would be better off without rain; or that since flames can burn, we would be happier without fire. Belief in a divine being is not our problem. Our problem is that we are so often unable to accept our differences.

– Madeleine K. Albright (formerly Secretary of State, United States), 2008

Terms and distinctions

There is an increasing need for teachers and other educators, particularly those with leadership and senior management responsibilities, to be 'religiously literate'. A crude measure of the need is the number of stories in the media that mention the words Christian and Muslim. In the *Guardian*, the word Christian appeared 770 times in 1985; 1,221 times in 1995; and 2,341 times in 2005. The word Muslim appeared 408 times in 1985; 1,106 times in 1995; and 2,114 times in 2005.

Religious literacy involves skills in understanding and assessing religious statements and behaviour; discerning the difference between valuable and harmful aspects of religion and religions; appreciating religious architecture, art, literature and music without necessarily accepting all the beliefs that they express or assume; and making reasonable accommodation between people holding different religious and non-religious worldviews.

The concept of religious literacy does not imply holding a set of distinctively religious beliefs, but rather implies understanding the range of ways in which religion may affect a person's values and perspectives. It implies also that a religious tradition should be understood in its own terms, so far as is possible, not through templates and assumptions derived from another tradition. For example, it is religiously illiterate to suppose that imams in Islam have the same range of roles and responsibilities as clerics in Christianity. Also, it is illiterate to equate an attack on a bishop of the established church with an attack on a cleric in a marginalised community subject to racist violence. It was religiously illiterate for a group of French writers, in connection with the controversy about the Danish caricatures in 2006, to defend them on the grounds that 'picking on the parish priest has long been a national sport'.

Religious literacy also involves recognising that within every tradition there is a tension and conversation between pressures to maintain the heritage and pressures to re-interpret it. It is religiously illiterate to suppose that all people with strong commitment to a certain tradition have much the same orientation

---

Reflections – 18

God on my side

I've learnt to hate Russians
All through my whole life
If another war starts
It's them we must fight
To hate them and fear them
To run and to hide
And accept it all bravely
With God on my side.

– Bob Dylan, 1960s

> ### Reflections – 19
> **Larger, freer and more loving**
>
> If the concept of God has any validity or any use, it can only be to make us larger, freer and more loving. If God cannot do this, then it is time we got rid of him.
>
> – *James Baldwin,* The Fire Next Time

towards it. Further, religious literacy involves understanding the pressures in every tradition that lead to the emergence of 'fundamentalism' and 'extremism', and that may cause people to use religious discourse to justify immoral acts, or patterns of inequality and unfair discrimination.

Conflicts, arguments and controversies exist not only between and within different religious traditions but also between religious traditions and secular ones. The latter include the worldviews implicit in the vast majority of social science, natural science, medicine, engineering, law and public administration, and in most contemporary work in the performing, literary and visual arts. Religious literacy includes understanding and taking seriously secular and humanist beliefs as well as religious ones.

> ### Reflections – 20
> **Open to the widest critique**
>
> I'm a great believer that the most important and most sustaining things in life are essentially irrational. Love, beauty, art, friendship, music, spirituality of whatever form, these things make no rational sense yet they are more important than any qualities that are rationally measurable. Those who think that, as they lie on their deathbed, they will be able to judge the success of their lives by how big a BMW they could afford at the end of it are in for a big surprise. However, it's their irrational nature that leaves religious beliefs wide open to interpretation, allowing occasionally practices to be established that are wholly contrary to the mores of a civilised, liberal society. Those practices must remain open to the widest critique, including what could be perceived as insult or abuse.
>
> – *Rowan Atkinson, 2008*

Religious affiliation can take a range of forms, and that a person may identify with a religious tradition without necessarily holding any distinctive theological views or engaging in any distinctive religious activities. For such people their religion provides markers of belonging rather than a set of beliefs. It's relevant to recall an old story from Northern Ireland. 'Are you a Protestant,' a visitor is asked, 'or a Catholic?' – 'Neither,' comes the reply, 'I'm an atheist.' – 'Yes, but are you a Protestant atheist or a Catholic atheist?'

Faith Equality: challenges for schools

■ **Reasonable adjustments**

Making alterations in routines and requirements, as and when reasonable, to accommodate the wishes, preferences and commitments of staff and pupils, and of parents and other carers.

■ **Visibility in the curriculum**

Including faith equality issues and positive images of people with a range of beliefs and worldviews in curriculum materials, modules and topics, wherever possible and appropriate.

■ **Handling disagreements**

Enabling staff and pupils to respect religious and non-religious views different from their own, but also to critique and challenge them when appropriate.

■ **Preventing and addressing bullying**

Using a range of measures to reduce and remove racist and religious harassment and bullying, and promoting positive attitudes and relationships between pupils of different religious and non-religious backgrounds.

■ **Allies**

Fostering and developing the qualities, skills, insights of allies – people who are not themselves targeted by religious bigotry but who through their actions and advocacy give moral, political and practical support to people who are.

■ **Action plans**

Creating and regularly reviewing plans for creating greater faith equality, and reporting on progress to governing bodies.

Gender

Legal and ethical context

The principal legislation in the UK is contained in the Sex Discrimination Act 1975, amended by the Equality Act 2006. There are further details on pages 87-8. A requirement particularly relevant to the education system is the need to address the causes of any differences between the pay of men and women related to their gender.

It is expected that new equalities legislation in 2009 will stipulate that issues of transgender should be treated as a distinct and therefore seventh equality strand. Guidance for schools on this topic can be accessed at the website of the Gender Identity Research and Education Society (www.gires.org.uk/).

Internationally, expectations and requirements relating to gender equality have been set out by a series of world conferences held about every five years since 1976. The Beijing Conference 1995 has been particularly influential.

Terms and distinctions

The terms *gender* and *sex* are frequently used interchangeably. For example, legislation in the UK is governed by the Sex Discrimination Act but contains a *gender* equality duty. In popular journalism, *sex* is almost invariably the term used in preference to gender. In academia, however, and in campaigns for equality between women and men, it has been increasingly customary to use the terms in two different ways.

Reflections – 21

Dream world

'Felicity certainly wants to leave school. And if she's to start on that typing course next year we ought to put her name down now.'

'I don't want Felicity to be a typist,' said Mor.

'Why not?' said Nan. 'She could have a good career. She could be secretary to some interesting man.'

'I don't want her to be secretary to some interesting man. I want her to be an interesting woman and have someone else to be her secretary.'

'You live in dream world...'

from The Sandcastle *by Iris Murdoch, 1950s*

When used differently, the term *sex* refers to a range of biological differences already present at a person's birth. The term *gender*, however, refers to differences that are not fixed in nature but are socially constructed and maintained in the course of someone's life by patterns of child-rearing and education, customs and conventions, divisions of labour, economic relationships and unequal distributions of power.

Gender Identity refers to the psychological identification of oneself as a boy or man or as a girl or woman. There is a presumption that this sense of identity will evolve along binary lines and be consistent with sexual appearance. For trans people, however, there is variance between their gender identity and their biological sex. As mentioned above, UK legislation is planned for 2009 that will make discrimination against trans people unlawful.

The United Nations Women's Conference in 2005 set out the following world-wide principles for promoting gender equality:

- there must be gender mainstreaming, to promote the empowerment of women and achieving gender equality by transforming structures of inequality

- full realisation of all human rights and fundamental freedoms is essential for the empowerment of women and girls

- full representation and full and equal participation of women is essential in political, social and economic decision-making and development policies

- the empowerment of women is a critical factor in the eradication of poverty

- men and boys share with women and girls joint responsibility for the promotion of gender equality

- states must prevent violence against women and girls and provide protection to the victims, and must investigate, prosecute and punish the perpetrators of violence against women and girls.

In the UK as in many countries there is are substantial disparities between women and men with regard to pay. One of the implications for schools is that

Reflections – 22

Just as their brothers do

Women are supposed to be very calm generally; but women feel just as men feel; they need exercise for their faculties, and a field for their efforts as much as their brothers do; they suffer from too rigid a restraint, too absolute a stagnation, precisely as men would suffer; and it is narrow-minded in their more privileged fellow-creatures to say that they ought to confine themselves to making puddings and knitting stockings, to playing on the piano and embroidering bags. It is thoughtless to condemn them, or laugh at them, if they seek to do more or learn more than custom has pronounced necessary for their sex.

(Charlotte Brontë, Jane Eyre, 19th century)

Reflections – 23

Violence and abuse

The British public gives more to a Devon-based donkey sanctuary than to the most prominent charities trying to combat violence and abuse against women, a report released today by a leading philanthropy watchdog reveals.

New Philanthropy Capital (NPC) has calculated that more than seven million women have been affected by domestic violence but found that Refuge, the Women's Aid Federation and Eaves Housing for Women have a combined annual income of just £17m. By contrast the Donkey Sanctuary, which has looked after 12,000 donkeys, received £20m in 2006.

NPC estimates the cost to society of domestic abuse, sexual violence, forced marriage, trafficking and honour crimes has reached £40bn a year – greater than the country's defence budget.

– news item, April 2008

positive measures need to be taken to enable girls to prepare for careers in science, engineering and technology. There are also disparities in relation to involvement in politics and public life generally. In this respect too, schools have responsibilities in the information, advice and guidance they give to girls.

A major issue in wider society that has practical implications for schools is violence against women (VAW).

Gender Equality: challenges in schools

■ Equality of outcome
Planning and implementing programmes which will close the gaps in achievement between girls and boys in science (including computer science), engineering, construction and technology, and in literacy-based subjects.

■ Visibility in the curriculum
Ensuring the inclusion of gender equality issues and positive images of both genders in curriculum materials, modules and topics, wherever possible and appropriate.

■ Preventing and addressing bullying
Using a range of measures to reduce and remove sexual harassment and bullying, and challenge trivialisation of violence against women.

■ Allies
Fostering and developing the qualities, skills and insights of allies – people who are not themselves targeted or affected by sexual harassment and gender stereotyping but who through their actions and advocacy give moral, political and practical support to those who are.

■ The public life of the school
Involving both girls and boys in the public life of the school.

■ Monitoring and review
Collecting and using a range of quantitative and qualitative evidence to show the extent and nature of progress towards greater gender equality.

■ Action plans
Creating and regularly reviewing plans for creating greater gender equality, and reporting on progress to governing bodies.

Sexuality

Legal and ethical background

Discrimination in employment and the provision of services on grounds of someone's sexuality, or assumed sexuality, is unlawful. With regard to employment, the principal legislation in the UK is contained in Employment Equality (sexual orientation) Regulations 2003. With regard to the provision of services it is contained in the Equality Act (Sexual Orientation) Regulations 2000. There is slightly fuller information on page 88.

The ethical principles underlying opposition to homophobia are the same as those which underpin opposition to other patterns of prejudice and discrimination. The patterns are present in schools as well as in wider society.

Terms and distinctions

The term *homophobia* was coined by the American psychologist George Weinberg in 1972, to refer to irrational fear of and opposition to same-sex relationships, and to prejudice against people who are, or who are believed to be, lesbian, gay, bisexual, transgender or questioning (LGBTQ). The term *heterosexism* was subsequently coined to refer to attitudes, assumptions and discrimination in favour of opposite-sex sexuality and relationships. It can include the presumption that everyone is straight or that opposite-sex attractions and relationships are the norm and therefore superior. The motives underlying homophobia and heterosexism include a desire for approval and acceptance from friends and peers, and a desire to ignore or downplay anxieties and insecurities about one's own sexuality or gender.

Amongst boys and men, homophobia is frequently connected with sexism and assumptions about masculinity. The concept of *sexuality-continuum* reflects the view that there is no strict hard-and-fast distinction between being straight and being lesbian or gay. The concept has been further developed to maintain that sexuality is multi-dimensional, as distinct from being a continuum, since it involves not only attraction and affection but also fantasies, relationships, life-styles and sense of identity, and that it may change over time.

Reflections – 24

A matter of ordinary justice

A student once asked me if I could have one wish granted to reverse an injustice, what would it be? I had to ask for two. One is for world leaders to forgive the debts of developing nations which hold them in such thrall. The other is for the world to end the persecution of people because of their sexual orientation, which is every bit as unjust as that crime against humanity, apartheid.

This is a matter of ordinary justice. We struggled against apartheid in South Africa, supported by people the world over, because black people were being blamed and made to suffer for something we could do nothing about – our very skins. It is the same with sexual orientation. It is a given. I could not have fought against the discrimination of apartheid and not also fight against the discrimination that homosexuals endure, even in our churches and faith groups.

And I am proud that in South Africa, when we won the chance to build our own new constitution, the human rights of all have been explicitly enshrined in our laws. My hope is that one day this will be the case all over the world, and that all will have equal rights. For me this struggle is a seamless rope. Opposing apartheid was a matter of justice. Opposing discrimination against women is a matter of justice. Opposing discrimination on the basis of sexual orientation is a matter of justice.

It is also a matter of love. Every human being is precious. We are all, all of us, part of God's family. We all must be allowed to love each other with honour.

– Archbishop Desmond Tutu, 2004

Reflections – 25

A matter of self-respect

For me, nothing could be taken for granted. I knew I was different long before I could attach it to sexuality at all. Like everybody else, sexuality is just one part of my personality, an important part, but not everything. I always struggled not to be reduced to just 'a gay activist' although there have been periods in my life when I have felt forced to speak out – as a matter of self-respect and survival.

– Lutz van Dijk, 2007

The history of legislative reform in the UK includes the Sexual Offences Act 1967, which partially decriminalised sex between men in England and Wales (it was not until 1980 and 1982 respectively that the same reform was introduced in Scotland and Northern Ireland); the lifting of the ban on lesbian women and gay men serving in the armed forces, 2000; the age of consent reduced to sixteen, 2000; the granting of equal rights to same-sex couples applying for adoption, 2002; section 146 of the Criminal Justice Act 2003 empowering courts to impose tougher sentences for offences aggravated or motivated by homophobic prejudice; and the Civil Partnership Act 2004.

In late 2008, 66 countries at the United Nations called for same-sex relationships to be decriminalised. Sixty other countries of the UN's 192 member states, including many in the Middle East and Africa, rejected the declaration. It is estimated that same-sex sexual relationships are in 2009 a criminal offence in more than 80 countries, and that in at least seven countries sex between men can be punished with the death penalty.

Reflections – 26

Endemic

Homophobic bullying is almost endemic in Britain's schools. Almost two thirds (65%) of young lesbian, gay and bisexual pupils have experienced direct bullying. Seventy five per cent of young gay people attending faith schools have experienced homophobic bullying.

Even if gay pupils are not directly experiencing bullying, they are learning in an environment where homophobic language and comments are commonplace. Ninety eight per cent of young gay people hear the phrases 'that's so gay' or 'you're so gay' in school, and over four fifths hear such comments often or frequently.

Ninety seven per cent of pupils hear other insulting homophobic remarks, such as 'poof', 'dyke', 'rug-muncher', 'queer' and 'bender'.

Less than a quarter (23%) of young gay people have been told that homophobic bullying is wrong in their school. In schools that have said homophobic bullying is wrong, gay young people are 60 per cent more likely not to have been bullied.

Over half of lesbian and gay pupils don't feel able to be themselves at school. Thirty five per cent of lesbian and gay pupils do not feel safe or accepted at school.

– from The School Report, Stonewall, 2006

Sexuality Equality: challenges for schools

Visibility in the curriculum
Including sexuality equality issues and positive images of gay and lesbian people in curriculum materials, modules and topics, wherever possible and appropriate.

Preventing and addressing bullying and harassment
Using a range of measures to reduce and remove harassment and bullying of gay and lesbian pupils, and promoting positive attitudes towards sexual diversity.

Allies
Fostering and developing the qualities, skills and insights of allies – people who are not themselves targeted or affected by homophobia but who through their actions and advocacy give moral, political and practical support to those who are.

Monitoring and review
Collecting and using a range of quantitative and qualitative evidence to show the extent and nature of progress towards sexuality equality.

World

Legal and ethical context

The national curriculum in England and Wales requires schools to teach about global interdependence – ecological, cultural, economic, political and moral.

International human rights standards require that all people, including children should learn about rights, and expect learning about rights not only through the content of the curriculum but also through the ways schools and classrooms are organised.

Since the world is interdependent, human beings have wider moral responsibilities than in the past. The global context in which all now live is the context in which the issues discussed on the pages of this book – age, class, cohesion, disability, ethnicity, faith, gender, sexuality – have to be considered.

Reflections – 27

Humankind

Be moved by
the state of
the world,
outspoken about
what's unfair, and excited
about making
a difference.
Be humankind.

– *Oxfam diary, 2009*

Terms and distinctions

Countries, cultures and communities are not cut off from each other. On the contrary, there has been much borrowing, mingling and mutual influence over the centuries between different countries and cultural traditions. Events and trends in one place in the modern world are frequently affected by events and trends elsewhere. You cannot understand your own local world close at hand without seeing it as part of a global system. You cannot take decisions in your own sphere of influence without there being implications and repercussions elsewhere.

Terms to refer to this relatively recent state of affairs include: global village, globalisation, one world, spaceship earth and interdependence. Terms to

---

Reflections – 28

The global tribe we have now become

Our ancestors have been human for a very long time. If a normal baby girl born forty thousand years ago were kidnapped by a time-traveller and raised in a normal family in New York, she would be ready for college in eighteen years. She would learn English (along with – who knows? – Spanish or Chinese), understand trigonometry, follow baseball and pop music; she would probably want a pierced tongue and a couple of tattoos. And she would be unrecognisably different from the brothers and sisters she left behind.

... Only in the past couple of centuries, as every human community has gradually been drawn into a single web of trade and a global network of information have we come to a point where each of us can realistically imagine contacting any other of our six billion conspecifics and sending that person something worth having: a radio, an antibiotic, a good idea. Unfortunately, we could also send, through negligence as easily as malice, things that will cause harm: a virus, an airborne pollutant, a bad idea. And the possibilities of good of ill are multiplied beyond measure when it comes to policies carried out by governments in our name.

Together, we can ruin poor farmers by dumping our subsidised grain into their markets, cripple industries by punitive tariffs, deliver weapons that will kill thousands on thousands.

Together, we can raise standards of living by adopting new policies on trade and aid, prevent or treat diseases with vaccines and pharmaceuticals, take measures against global climate change, encourage resistance to tyranny and concern for the worth of each human life.

... Each person you know about and can affect is someone to whom you have responsibilities; to say this is just to affirm the very idea of morality. The challenge, then, is to take hearts and minds formed over the long millennia of living in local troops and equip them with ideas and institutions that will allow us to live together as the global tribe that we have become..

Kwame Anthony Appiah, 2006

describe the implications for education include global citizenship and cosmopolitanism.

In recent years, Unicef has developed the Rights Respecting Schools project in countries across the world. Schools which have engaged with the project report:

- improved pupil self-esteem
- enhanced moral development
- improved behaviour and relationships
- more positive attitudes towards diversity in society
- enhanced discussion and decision-making skills and greater willingness to solve problems through negotiation rather than force
- increased global awareness
- reduction of prejudice
- active citizenship, locally, nationally and globally
- greater interest in affairs and events in other countries
- less bullying and truancy
- more readiness by pupils to be assertive in intervening and mediating in conflicts and quarrels
- increased insight into the nature of rules and negotiated agreements, readiness to accept and take responsibility for upholding standards of civility and fairness
- greater job-satisfaction for teachers..

Reflections – 29

Where to begin?

Where, after all, do universal human rights begin? In small places, close to home – so close and so small that they cannot be seen on any maps of the world. Yet they are the world of the individual person; the neighbourhood he lives in; the school or college he attends; the factory, farm, or office where he works. Such are the places where every man, woman, and child seeks equal justice, equal opportunity, equal dignity without discrimination. Unless these rights have meaning there, they have little meaning anywhere.

Eleanor Roosevelt, 1958

Reflections – 30

All children

My hope is that whatever you do to make a good life for yourself — whether you become a teacher, or social worker, or business person, or lawyer, or poet, or scientist — you will devote part of your life to making this a better world for your children, for all children. My hope is that your generation will demand an end to war, that your generation will do something that has not yet been done in history and wipe out the national boundaries that separate us from other human beings on this earth.

– Howard Zinn, speech on graduation day at Spelman College 15 May 2005

Reflections – 31

Suspicion

Being British is about driving in a German car containing African metals to an Irish pub for a Belgian beer, then grabbing a Bengali curry or a Turkish kebab on the way home, to sit on Swedish furniture and watch an American show on a Japanese TV. And the most British thing of all? Suspicion of anything foreign.

– source unknown

The World: challenges for schools

Preparing children and young people for change, complexity and uncertainty, but enabling them to feel at the same time that they need not to be passive and are not powerless.

Teaching about the relationships between global and local issues.

Teaching about issues which require international cooperation, for example world poverty, sustainable development, climate change and human rights.

Helping children and young people to see themselves not only as citizens of their own country but also as world citizens.

Making links with schools in other countries.

Community Cohesion: challenges for schools

helping pupils come to understand others, value diversity, develop shared values, appreciate human rights and apply and defend them, and develop skills in participation and responsible action, removing barriers to access and participation in learning, and working to eliminate different outcomes for various groups in relation to, for example, class, disability, ethnicity and gender

providing reasonable means for pupils, their friends and families to interact with people from backgrounds different from their own, and build positive relations

enabling all pupils to feel that they belong to their school, and collecting quantitative and qualitative evidence to check the extent to which this aim is being achieved

enabling pupils from a range of backgrounds to take part in the public life of the school

enabling pupils to develop skills in handling disagreements and conflicts

showing respect for the identities and mixed loyalties of all parents and other carers, and all pupils and staff

engaging with the school's local neighbourhood

ensuring school leadership teams have a shared understanding of the duty to promote community cohesion, a soundly based knowledge of the school's local community and, through incisive analysis, a strategy for contributing effectively to cohesion.

Part Two
Bringing the strands together: connections and similarities

This section of the book considers the strands of equality and diversity as a single entity, emphasising the features they all have in common.

Similarities and connections

In the first section of this book, each strand of equality and diversity was considered separately. Now, the strands are considered all together, as if they were a single entity. First, there is a summary of similarities. On later pages several of the similarities are considered in greater detail.

Similarity 1
All people benefit

Think ramps, those architectural features that facilitate access to public buildings for people using wheel-chairs. When these were first required by law, there was a certain amount of muttering about political correctness. Was it really defensible, people asked, to spend so much money on items that would benefit only a small numerical minority, those who use wheel-chairs?

But actually, of course, ramps are of great value to lots of other people as well – parents, grandparents and other carers with infants in buggies, and anyone with a heavy suitcase on wheels, and anyone temporarily affected by a sprained ankle, or feeling a bit weary. Everyone also benefits from ramps in a rather invisible or philosophical way. For ramps subliminally remind people every time they see one, regardless of whether they actually use it, that they live in a society that recognises, accommodates and welcomes difference – not just differences of mobility but many other kinds of difference as well. Everyone benefits from living in such a society, for everyone belongs to a minority of one sort or another.

And in the other strands too, adjustments made for a numerical or powerless minority are of potential or actual benefit for the majority as well. For example, adjustments to teaching methods to accommodate pupils for whom English is an additional language are likely to help all pupils develop the academic skills they need. Measures to promote gender equality are of benefit to boys as well as girls, and measures to promote sexuality equality are likely to develop sensitivity and self-awareness in all people, including those who are straight. The social model of disability (see pages 8-9), appropriately modified, is relevant for a wide range of situations and contexts. On its website the Centre for Studies on Inclusive Education (CSIE) quotes the co-director of the Centre for Equity in Education at the University of Manchester: 'A detailed consideration of the barriers experienced by some pupils can help us to develop forms of schooling that will be more effective for all pupils.'

Similarity 2
Underlying principles

The same generic principles apply to all strands. This is demonstrated on pages 26-28.

Similarity 3
Dealing with prejudice-related bullying and incidents

In all strands there is a duty to address and prevent bullying and harassment, and to promote positive relationships and attitudes. This is considered on pages 29-34.

Similarity 4
Allies

With regard to all the strands it is important to foster and develop the qualities, skills and insights of allies – people who are not themselves directly affected by disadvantage, inequality and discrimination but who ,through their actions and advocacy, give moral, political and practical support to those who are.

Similarity 5
The relationship between prejudice, discrimination and exclusion

With all the strands it is important to make a distinction between prejudice and discrimination, for you do not necessarily address the one by addressing the other. Neither prejudice nor discrimination is the same as exclusion. These matters are considered further in the boxes on page 25.

Similarity 6
Classroom methods and practical approaches

All the strands have in common that there are implications not only for what is taught but also for how it is taught. This is discussed on pages 37-41.

Similarity 7
Language and political correctness

In all the strands there are concerns to develop the most appropriate language to describe reality and perceptions, and there are worries about so-called political correctness. This is considered on pages 42-45.

Similarity 8
Issues of identity, and 'me-first' and 'us-first'

All the strands necessarily involve feelings about, and understandings of, people different from oneself. They also, therefore, involve feelings and understandings about one's own identity and about the nature of the groups to which one belongs. Such self-understandings frequently involve mixed loyalties. In educational settings it is frequently more important, in the first instance, to consider one's own identity rather than that of others – 'us' rather than 'them'. By the same token, there is often a need for single-identity groups – women-only groups and shortlists, for example, and single-sex teaching groups.

Similarity 9
Challenges for schools

With regard to each strand of equality and diversity there is much the same set of challenges. A composite list of challenges, drawn and adapted from the first part of this book, is shown on page 24.

Similarity 10
Whole-school management and leadership

All the strands of equality and diversity depend on clear, explicit and robust leadership. For example, addressing the challenges listed on page 24 requires the attention and active, visible involvement of all members of a school's senior leadership team. There is a summary in a later section of the book (pages 82-85) of action points for leadership teams and governing bodies to consider.

Equality and diversity: generic challenges for schools

■ **Equality of outcome**

Planning and implementing programmes which will close the gaps in achievement between relevant groups, and increase the participation of under-represented groups in higher and further education.

■ **Equality of participation**

Planning and implementing programmes which will close the gaps in participation, for example increasing the participation of girls in science and mathematics, and the participation of boys in literacy-bases subjects.

■ **Equality of belonging**

Enabling all pupils to feel they belong to their school, are known and respected, and have a stake in the school's wellbeing and flourishing.

■ **Visibility in the curriculum**

Including equality and diversity issues and positive images of under-represented groups in curriculum materials, modules and topics, wherever possible and appropriate.

■ **Understanding**

Ensuring all members of the school community understand the requirements of legislation, and also certain essential concepts, for example the social model of disability and the conceptual differences between prejudice and discrimination, sex and gender, and colour and cultural racism.

■ **Preventing and addressing bullying and harassment**

Using a range of measures to reduce and remove prejudice-related harassment and bullying, and promoting positive attitudes towards people different from oneself.

■ **Involvement**

Ensuring that members of under-represented groups are involved in the design and implementation of measures and projects intended to be of benefit of them – 'nothing about us without us' – and listening to their views and voices.

■ **Allies**

Fostering and developing the qualities, skills and insights of allies – people who are not themselves directly affected by disadvantage, inequality and discrimination but who, through their actions and advocacy, give moral, political and practical support to those who are.

■ **The public life of the school**

Involving pupils with a wide range of backgrounds and characteristics in the public life of the school.

■ **Whole-school approaches**

Ensuring senior leadership teams and governing bodies give a strong and explicit lead, both in written documents, in oral communications of various kinds, and in their presence at, and participation in, significant events.

■ **Monitoring and review**

Collecting and using a range of quantitative and qualitative evidence, and maintaining a robust information base, to show the extent and nature of progress towards greater equality.

■ **Action plans**

Creating and regularly reviewing plans for creating greater equality, and reporting on progress to governing bodies.

The ABC of prejudice, discrimination and exclusion

With all the strands of equality and diversity, it is helpful to distinguish between a) prejudice b) discrimination and c) exclusion. Or between, with different words:

A. **attitudes and assumptions**, expressed through stories, narratives and discourse, for example text, talk and imagery in the media, and in everyday conversation. The stories, narratives and discourse are to do with views of the self and the other – 'us' and 'them'. They are summarised in Table 2.

B. **behaviour**, including not only discrimination in employment and the provision of services but also violence, harassment and criminal damage.

C. **context of exclusion and inequality**, including unequal outcomes and unequal participation in society.

Common sense tends to suppose there is a simple chain of cause and effect between prejudice, discrimination and exclusion. Negative attitudes, it is imagined, lead to discriminatory behaviours and these in their turn result in unequal distributions of power and resources. This widely held view is particularly popular amongst teachers and lecturers in the education system, in so far as we imagine that our primary task is the formation of individual hearts and minds, since it reassuringly implies society still needs us. The common sense view is shown schematically in Figure 3.1

Figure 3.1: A commonsense view of cause and effect

Prejudice ⟶ Discrimination ⟶ Exclusion

However, common sense is here, as so often elsewhere, a simplistic and insufficient guide. More complex relationships between cause and effect in relation to inequality need to be considered, for each of the three main components in Figure 3.1 is both cause and consequence of each of the others, as visualised in Figure 3.2.

Figure 3.2: A more complex view of cause and effect

Prejudice ⟷ Discrimination
Prejudice ⟷ Exclusion
Discrimination ⟷ Exclusion

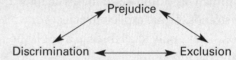

The two-way arrows in Figure 3 recall, for example, the well-known dictum that 'slavery was not born of racism. Rather, racism was the consequence of slavery.' Similarly in the other strands and dimensions of the equalities agenda: attitudes, stories, stereotypes and mental maps can derive from the desire to explain, justify and perpetuate unequal power relations and discriminatory practices, but they are not themselves the cause of discrimination and inequalities.

Source: adapted from The Future of Multi-Ethnic Britain*, 2000*

Principles underlying legislation

Introductory

Legislation about equality and diversity in Great Britain is concerned with six separate strands or areas:

- age
- disability
- ethnicity
- faith, religion or belief
- gender, including gender reassignment
- sexuality

The ten principles summarised in this chapter apply to all six strands. All are explicit in at least one piece of legislation. They apply to all three of a public body's three principal functions:

- as a provider of services and resources
- as an employer
- as a purchaser.

The exact wording in the various pieces of legislation is shown on pages 86-88. Where the wording here is different from the wording in legislation, this is explained on pages 42-45. The chapter is based on guidance issued by the Department for Children, Schools and Families in connection with equality impact assessments (EQUIAs).

Principle 1: EQUALITY
All people are of equal value and should be treated with equal respect, dignity and consideration.

- ☐ whatever their age
- ☐ whether or not they are disabled
- ☐ whatever their ethnicity, culture, national origin or national status
- ☐ whatever their faith tradition, religion or belief
- ☐ whichever their gender
- ☐ whatever their sexual identity

PRINCIPLE 2: DIFFERENCE AND REASONABLE ACCOMMODATION
People have a range of different interests, needs and experiences

Treating people equally (Principle 1) does not necessarily mean treating them all the same. Policies, procedures and activities must not discriminate, but also must take account of differences of experience, outlook and background – one size does not 'fit all'. In particular policies must take account of the kinds of specific barrier, inequality and disadvantage which people may face, and must make reasonable adjustments and accommodation in relation to:

- ☐ age
- ☐ disability
- ☐ ethnicity, so that different cultural backgrounds and experiences of racism are recognised
- ☐ faith traditions, religion or belief
- ☐ gender, so that different needs and experiences are recognised
- ☐ sexual identity

Principle 3: COHESION
Positive attitudes, relationships and interaction should be fostered, and a shared sense of cohesion and belonging. Therefore, hate-crime and prejudice-related incidents and harassment should be addressed and prevented.

Policies, procedures and activities should promote:

- ☐ mutually positive attitudes between older people and younger, and mutually beneficial relationships
- ☐ positive attitudes towards disabled people, good relations between disabled and non-disabled people, and an absence of harassment of disabled people
- ☐ positive interaction, good relations and dialogue between groups and communities different from each other in terms of ethnicity, culture, national origin or national status, and an absence of racism-related bullying and incidents

☐ mutual respect and good relations between girls and boys, and women and men, and an absence of sexual harassment and bullying

☐ positive interaction, good relations and dialogue between groups and communities different from each other in terms of faith tradition, religion or belief, and an absence of racism-related bullying and incidents

☐ good relations between people regardless of their sexual identity, and an absence of homophobic incidents and bullying

Principle 4: BEING PROACTIVE TO CREATE GREATER EQUALITY OF OUTCOME
Opportunities should be taken to reduce and remove inequalities of outcome and the barriers that already exist, with a view to producing not only equality of opportunity but also equality of outcome.

It is not enough just to avoid discrimination and negative impacts. In addition to avoiding or minimising possible negative impacts of our policies, we must take opportunities to maximise positive impacts by reducing and removing inequalities and barriers that may already exist between:

☐ people of different ages

☐ disabled and non-disabled people

☐ people of different ethnic and cultural backgrounds

☐ girls and boys, women and men

☐ people from different faith traditions

☐ people with different sexual identities

Principle 5: CONSULTATION AND INVOLVEMENT
People affected by a policy or activity should be consulted and involved in the design of new policies, and in the review of existing ones – 'nothing about us without us'.

Views and voices should be collected, directly and through representative bodies, from:

☐ people of all ages

☐ disabled people as well as non-disabled

☐ people from a range of ethnic and cultural backgrounds

☐ people from different faith traditions

☐ both women and men, and girls and boys

☐ people with a range of sexual identities

Principle 6: PARTICIPATION
All people should be enabled to take a full part in economic, political, social and cultural life at local and national levels.

Policies and activities should benefit society as a whole, both locally and nationally, by fostering greater participation in public life, and in the affairs of voluntary and community sector organisations and institutions. This applies to:

☐ people of all ages

☐ disabled people as well as non-disabled

☐ people from a range of ethnic and cultural backgrounds

☐ people from different faith traditions

☐ both women and men, and girls and boys

☐ people with a range of sexual identities

Principle 7: EVIDENCE
Policies should be based on reliable evidence

When new policies are proposed, and existing policies are monitored and reviewed, a range of quantitative and qualitative evidence should be collected and used about the likely impact on:

- ☐ people of all ages
- ☐ disabled people as well as non-disabled
- ☐ people from a range of ethnic and cultural backgrounds
- ☐ people from different faith traditions
- ☐ both women and men, and girls and boys
- ☐ people with a range of sexual identities

Principle 8: COMPLEXITY
All people have multiple identities.

No one is just one thing. All have a range of different affiliations and loyalties. Many of the terms and categories used in the equalities field are necessarily imprecise and have the potential to be misleading. This is true of:

- ☐ people of all ages
- ☐ disabled people as well as non-disabled
- ☐ people from a range of ethnic and cultural backgrounds
- ☐ people from different faith traditions
- ☐ both women and men, and girls and boys
- ☐ people with a range of sexual identities

Principle 9: SOCIAL CLASS
The inequalities cited above in respect to age, ethnicity, disability, faith, gender and sexuality should not be considered independently of inequalities of social class.

Differences of wealth, income, occupation, status, educational qualifications, influence, leisure activities, consumption patterns, health levels, aspirations and outlooks are relevant when we are designing, implementing and improving services for:

- ☐ people of all ages
- ☐ disabled people as well as non-disabled
- ☐ people from a range of ethnic and cultural backgrounds
- ☐ people from different faith traditions
- ☐ both women and men, and both girls and boys
- ☐ people with a range of sexual identities

Principle 10: ACTION
Principles are not enough. There must also be action.

Every public body must draw up an action plan or delivery plan showing the specific measures it will adopt to create greater equality in its sphere of influence in relation to:

- ■ disability
- ■ ethnicity
- ■ gender, including gender identity

Ideally the plan should also cover:

- ■ age
- ■ faith, religion and belief
- ■ sexual identity

Prejudice-related bullying and behaviour

Definition

The term *prejudice-related bullying* refers to a range of hurtful behaviour, physical or emotional or both, which causes someone to feel powerless, worthless, excluded or marginalised, and which is connected with prejudices around belonging, identity and equality in wider society – in particular, prejudices to do with

- disabilities and special educational needs
- ethnic, cultural and religious backgrounds
- gender
- home life, for example in relation to issues of care, parental occupation, poverty and social class
- sexual identity.

Reflections – 32

Just call them something back

We were bussed to a faraway school,'where we were the only children with brown faces. When we got called names the teachers would say: 'Oh just call them something back like milky.'

Anila Baig, 2007

The following aspects of prejudice-related bullying should be borne in mind:

- Pupils at the receiving end experience great distress. They may become fearful, depressed and lacking in self-confidence, and reluctant to attend school. Their progress at school may be severely damaged. Their distress is connected with feelings of being left out, invisible, excluded, unvalued, rejected.

- Those who engage or collude in bullying develop a false pride in their own superiority.

- Teachers and even parents are sometimes unaware of the miseries that are being inflicted, or of the cruelty that is being perpetrated.

- Girls and boys engage in bullying in different ways.

- When dealing with incidents, staff must attend to a) the needs, feelings and wishes of pupils at the receiving end b) the needs, feelings and wishes of their parents and carers c) the children and young people principally responsible for the bullying d) any supporters they have and e) any bystanders and witnesses.

- Prejudices have a long history, affecting millions of people and are a common feature in wider society. People are seriously harmed and injured by them, and sometimes even viciously attacked and murdered. Words such Spotty, Ginger, Fatty and Four Eyes are seldom used by adults and seldom if ever used by adults to justify offensive behaviour. Forms of prejudice-related bullying, however, are associated with discrimination in employment and the provision of services, and with a range of criminal offences. Children and young children do not, it follows, necessarily 'grow out of' them.

- There is tacit or even explicit support for certain prejudices in the tabloid press, in radio phone-in programmes and in some television. In particular there is support for prejudices against Muslim people, Travellers and Gypsies, people seeking asylum, and people who are gay, lesbian or bisexual.

- The distinctive feature of a prejudice-related attack or insult is that a person is attacked or insulted not as an individual, as in most other offences, but as the representative of a family, community or group. Other members of the same group, family or community are in consequence made to feel threatened and intimidated as well. So it is not just the pupil who is attacked who feels unwelcome or marginalised. 'When they call me a Paki,' explains nine-year-old Sereena, 'it's not just me they're hurting. It's all my family and all other black people too.'

- Or for example all women are intimidated if a single woman is attacked in a lonely place; all disabled people feel threatened and reluctant to go out into public spaces when they hear of an attack on a single disabled individual; all gay, lesbian and bisexual people have their liberty of movement curtailed by an attack on an individual who is believed to be non-heterosexual.

- Prejudice-related words and behaviour are experienced as attacks on the values, loyalties and commitments central to a person's sense of identity and self-worth. Often, therefore, they hurt not only more widely but also more deeply. 'They attack me for being an Arab,' remarks Ahmed. 'But I'm an Arab because my father is an Arab, and I love my father. Do they think I should stop loving my father? I couldn't do that, ever.' In an analogous way, attacks on gay, lesbian or bisexual people are experienced as attacks not only on one person but also on friends, lovers and partners, and the LGBT community.

- Prejudice-related attacks are committed not only against a community but also, in the eyes of offenders themselves, on behalf of a community – they see themselves as 'normal', and as representative of, and supported in, their behaviour by their friends, family and peer group, and they may well feel it is right and proper to take the law into their own hands.

- Quite apart from whether those responsible see themselves as representatives of their own community, taking the law into their own hands, this is how they may be seen by those at the receiving end. So a disabled child, for example, may then fear and distrust all non-disabled people, not just those who engage in bullying.

- Most bullying or harassment involves a series of incidents over time. In the case of prejudice-related bullying, however, a single one-off incident may have precisely the same impact as a series of incidents over time. This is because it may be experienced by the person at the receiving end as part of a general pattern of prejudiced hostility. It can in consequence be every bit as intimidating, rejecting and hurtful as a series of events over time.

- In the case of homophobic bullying, the person under attack may or may not be gay, lesbian or bisexual, or may be uncertain about their sexuality. Coming out to a teacher about their sexuality or uncertainty may be stressful, and the response by the teacher may require considerable sensitivity to give appropriate support and advice.

Approaches to bullying and harassment

There are four broad approaches to dealing with bullying and harassment: dismissive, punitive, corrective and transformative. These are discussed below.

Approach 1
Dismissive

Ignoring or making light of an incident is seldom if ever appropriate. It permits the pupil principally responsible for the bullying – and also his or her friends and associates, and any witnesses and bystanders – to assume there's nothing wrong with their behaviour. The behaviour may therefore be repeated.

Also, and even more seriously, this approach gives no support to those at the receiving end. They may in consequence assume teachers and the school generally are indifferent to issues of prejudice and hostility in the school and in society, and will not bother to complain if there are further incidents. They may also feel that the school does not care for them, does not understand their experiences and perceptions, does not see them as fully belonging. Feelings of being excluded and worthless, caused by the bullying, will then be exacerbated, and a picture builds up of the whole school being insensitive and uncaring.

Approach 2
Punitive

Children and young people responsible for bullying and any onlookers must be in no doubt that their behaviour is unacceptable, and those at the receiving end of bullying must similarly be in no doubt they are supported by the school. But if expressions of disapproval and punishments are used in isolation, and not complemented by teaching and learning about the reasons why prejudice-related bullying is wrong, they may feed the recepient's bitterness and sense of not being understood. Such bitterness may then be expressed elsewhere, away from the school's awareness.

Approach 3
Corrective

It is important that teachers should explain why prejudice is wrong, and that they should correct ignorant views and prejudices by giving facts, statistics and rational arguments. This is likely to involve deconstructing specific lines of thought, pointing out contradictions and inconsistencies, and showing that even when a factual statement is true ('They own all the corner shops round here') it does not logically justify harassment, abuse or violence. Correction is also likely to involve challenging over-generalisations.

But, like expressions of disapproval and punishments, intellectual arguments may feed bitterness and a sense of not being understood. Pupils may feel an increased sense of personal inferiority and powerlessness, and greater resentment of authority. They may become *more* prejudiced in their attitudes and behaviour rather than less. They may then be readily attracted to claims by organisations such as the British National Party and by some newspapers that the country is being destroyed by 'the political correctness brigade'.

Approach 4
Restorative

In general terms, the primary objectives of a transformative approach are to:

■ attend fully to the emotional and social needs of those who are at the receiving end of bullying, and of those who are close to them

■ prevent re-offending by enabling offenders to assume active responsibility for their actions and by reintegrating them into the school community

■ avoid escalation, and mounting expense of time and energy

■ repair and recreate the community that has been damaged by the bullying, with a view to making it more active in preventing more bullying in the future.

The essential purpose of the restorative approach is to put right the wrongs and harms that have been caused. It does this by:

■ focusing on the harms and consequent needs of those at the receiving end, as well as the harms and needs of the community and of offenders

■ addressing the obligations that arise from those harms, particularly the obligations of the offender and of the wider community

■ using inclusive, collaborative processes

■ involving all stakeholders, including not only those at the receiving end and those responsible, but also parents and friends, audiences and bystanders, and the wider community.

The differences between punitive and restorative approaches are shown in Table 3.0

Table 3: Differences between punitive justice and restorative justice

Key questions	Punitive justice	Restorative justice
What is crime?	A violation of the law and the state	A violation of people and relationships
What do violations create?	Guilt	Needs and obligations
What should be the central focus?	Offenders getting what they deserve	The needs of those who have been hurt and the obligations of offenders to repair harm
What does justice require?	That those who are guilty should be identified and punished.	That victims, offenders and the community should work together to put things right

Source: adapted slightly from Howard Zehr (2002)

When designing and using restorative approaches to prejudice-related bullying, harassment and abuse, it is relevant to bear in mind the following:

■ Prejudiced beliefs and behaviour in young people have their sources in anxieties about identity and territory, and in desires to belong to a sub-culture of peers or a gang where racism, sexism, homophobia and hostility towards disabled people are some (but usually not all) of the principal features.

■ Those who are responsible, it follows, often operate as a group rather than as single individuals, and teachers need to engage not only with those most obviously responsible but also with witnesses, bystanders, audiences and supporters. This point is illustrated in the diagram below.

■ Teachers should show they understand the anxieties and desires which children and young people have around identity, belonging and self-esteem, and do their best to engage with them.

■ All pupils should be involved in dealing with prejudice-related incidents, for example through peer mediation activities. It is not just a matter for adults.

■ Both as individuals and as staffs, teachers need to have a shared philosophy about the nature of a diverse society, and about how to deal with conflicts, controversies and difference in it.

■ There should be attention to preventing and reducing prejudice-related bullying through the curriculum (particularly, but by no means only, the citizenship and PSHE curriculum) and in a school's overall ethos. This point is illustrated at length in part 3 of this book, pages 47-75.

The four approaches to dealing with incidents – dismissive, punitive, corrective, restorative – can be clarified and illustrated with reference to real or imagined incidents. With each incident, discussion can be of four matters – though these are interlinked:

■ the background, namely what you think may have happened beforehand, both immediately and over time

■ the follow-up, distinguishing between the next few minutes, the next few days, the next few weeks

■ the issues which the story raises – How? Why? What? When?

■ the implications and action points for your own work situation.

Incidents for such discussion include those which are listed opposite. All are based on real events.

BULLYING IN SCHOOLS – A DIAGRAMMATIC SUMMARY OF THE PARTS PUPILS PLAY

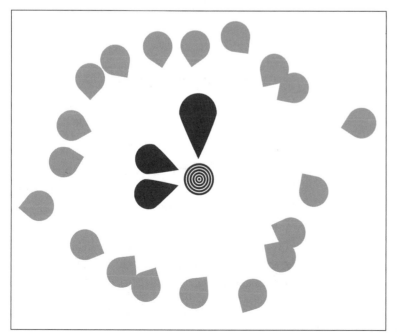

In much bullying in schools there is a range of roles that pupils may play. Most pupils take the part of bystanders – by not intervening they give the bullying their tacit approval. In the diagram above, they are shown standing around in a loose circle. In the middle of the circle there is the ringleader or chief bully, reinforced by two key supporters ('hench-persons'). Also in the middle there is the person at the receiving end of the bullying, targeted both by the ringleader and by the ringleader's two supporters. Outside the circle there are two figures. The diagram shows one who is walking away, hopefully to obtain help from a teacher. The other is coming towards the circle, hopefully to confront the bullies and to stand up for the person being targeted.

Source: Racist Incidents and Bullying in Schools *by Robin Richardson and Berenice Miles, Trentham Books, 2008.*

Incidents for discussion

Used to it

Someone of Sri Lankan background has recently taken over a local shop. He mentions in conversation with a teacher that he gets a lot of low-level racist abuse from certain pupils at the school. He's used to it, he says, and doesn't want to make a formal complaint.

Doesn't appear to mind

A girl from Poland has recently joined the class. She is addressed as Pollywog by a group of other girls and doesn't appear to mind.

Retaliates

Geoffrey, who is of Traveller heritage, has annoyed Darren. Darren retaliates with anger, calling him 'Pikey'.

You're all the same

A girl comes home in tears reporting that other pupils have said to her: 'You Jews are terrible, you're all the same. You're murderers. Why are you killing thousands of people in Palestine? Why don't you leave other people alone?'

My dad agrees

In an RE lesson a pupil produces a leaflet published by the British National Party.

'We owe it to our children to defend our Christian culture,' it says. And: 'Are you concerned about the growth of Islam in Britain?' The pupil says: 'My dad agrees with this. Do you, miss?'

White bitch

Pupils are queuing up in the canteen at lunchtime waiting. There's some pushing and shoving and a girl is pushed into another girl, knocking her tray out of her hands. The girl whose tray has been knocked turns to the other girl and calls her a white bitch.

I feel they don't like me

'No-one's ever called me a nasty name,' a pupil tells a teacher, 'but all the same I feel the other girls don't like me, and I think they're spreading rumours about me. I think it's because of my colour.'

Same as most teachers

'You only ever pick on black or Asian kids,' says a pupil to a teacher. 'You're racist, that's why, same as most white people.'

Cheerfully

Boys are playing football in the playground. Whenever someone fumbles a pass or misses a tackle the others cheerfully rebuke him with words such as poof, gay, fairy and wanker. Also, they are heard calling each other Nigger and Paki.

Easy to understand

In a citizenship lesson students note discrepancies in the take-home pay of women and men. 'It's easy to understand,' says someone. 'Girls are basically no good at the kinds of job that are well-paid. Or else they have babies and stuff and can't work as hard.'

Rather die

A girl gets teased because, say others, she's fat and will never get a boyfriend. 'I'll starve myself,' she tells a teacher. 'I'd rather die than put up with any more of this.'

Daren't tell anyone

The school has a system for receiving anonymous messages about problems and concerns. 'I'm gay,' writes someone. 'But I daren't tell anyone.'

Overheard

A colleague is overheard rebuking a group of boys who are talking together when they should be getting on with their work. 'You lot,' says the colleague, 'stop behaving like a bunch of girls'.

Graffiti

Graffiti appears on a wall near the school: 'Death to all poofs and lezzas'.

Nothing wrong?

A parent reports that her son has become miserable and withdrawn recently and that it seems to be connected with emails and text messages he has been receiving. He maintains, however, there's nothing wrong.

Just a phase?

'I told my mother I'm gay,' says a girl. 'She said it's just a phase I'm going through and I'll get over it once I have a boyfriend.'

On the bus

A girl tells a teacher she frequently gets touched sexually by boys on a school bus and when she says she doesn't like it and tells them to stop they call her a dyke. Other girls on the bus don't defend her, but say they suspect she fancies them and they need to keep away from her.

Prejudice-related bullying in schools – some frequently asked questions

What is the legal requirement?
Currently, the law requires schools to keep a record of racist incidents and to send a periodic report to their local authority (LA).

On 26 September 2008 DCSF ministers announced that the recording of all bullying was to be made compulsory.

Why report to the local authority?
We use the data to carry out our statutory responsibilities. We provide an annual report for our own Members, and for governing bodies of schools. Normal rules of confidentiality apply. We only use aggregated data to inform our reporting and planning processes

Why go beyond the legal minimum?
We acknowledge that schools may want to go beyond the legal requirement and keep a record not only of incidents connected with race, culture and ethnicity, but also those connected with other kinds of prejudice – including sexual harassment, bullying of pupils with disabilities and special needs, and homophobic bullying.

This will provide valuable information that will inform the school's own self-evaluation.

Under the Every Child Matters agenda governing bodies and local authorities need to be confident that learners feel safe and adopt safe practices. This includes feeling safe from bullying, particularly forms of bullying which reflect prejudices in wider society.

The additional information will enable each individual school to ensure it has a clear and informed view as to the extent of prejudice-related bullying. Schools can then plan more effectively to make improvements.

Monitoring of incidents and bullying around many forms of prejudice, not racial prejudice only, is increasingly important with new legal requirements coming into force nationally relating to disability, faith or religion, gender and sexual orientation.

It is easier to explain to children and young people why racist bullying is hurtful and therefore wrong if we also explain why bullying around gender, disability and sexuality is hurtful and wrong.

Should schools aim for a nil return to the LA on racist bullying?
No: a school's population does not exist in a vacuum away from the rest of society, nor is it unchanging. It would be unrealistic for any school to expect that no prejudice-related bullying will ever take place. A nil return from a school might imply that pupils are not confident about reporting incidents to staff, or that staff have not understood the nature or seriousness of prejudice-related incidents.

Do we have to record small, insignificant incidents?
Ideally, yes. Every incident, no matter how seemingly small, should be recorded and dealt with. If offenders and onlookers are permitted to believe that prejudice-related bullying is acceptable they may become involved later in serious criminal or unlawful activity.

In the new scheme we are introducing we recognise distinctions between different levels of seriousness. We expect that this will be more helpful than simply lumping together all incidents, regardless of how malicious they may be, and of how much hurt they cause.

'Incidents' or 'bullying'?
The legal requirement is to collect data on racist '*incidents*'. The term came into education in this context from policing. It is often appropriate and useful. But usually the behaviour to be challenged is more accurately described as bullying. This has been emphasised at length by the DCSF through its website on countering racist bullying.

It may be contended that 'incidents' are one-off whereas 'bullying' involves a series of incidents over time. But from the point of view of a child or young person at the receiving end, what looks like a one-off incident to a teacher may well be experienced as part of a pattern, and likely to be repeated.

Source: adapted from a document issued in Derbyshire, 2008

Big ideas across the curriculum

Introductory notes

'What's the big idea?' This a key question in curriculum planning – what are the essential generalisations we intend to present and to communicate, the key concepts we want pupils to understand and make their own? There are notes here on six sets of big ideas, as listed below. The ideas are connected to each other and overlap but can be separated and given names, for the sake of convenience. They are as follows:

- shared humanity
- identity, belonging and difference
- globalisation and the global village
- learning from other places and times
- conflict resolution and justice
- open and closed minds.

These ideas can be taught in all subjects and at all ages. They can be taught through a school's general ethos and atmosphere, not just formally and directly through what used to be called chalk and talk. Also, they can be taught through the illustrative material to which reference is made in skills-based subjects.

Shared humanity

Human beings belong to a single race, the human race. At all times in history and in all cultural traditions, they have certain basic tasks, problems, aspirations and needs in common – there is a shared humanity. Because all have the same underlying humanity, all are of equal value. All should be treated fairly and all should have the same basic human rights.

Art, drama, history, music, novels, poetry, religion and stories all explore humankind's basic humanity. In science, pupils learn about aspects of human biology that are universal, about universals in the inorganic world and about science as a universal human activity. Universals in biology are also encountered in health education and PE. In geography, pupils learn about recurring patterns in relationships between human beings and their physical environment.

Identity, belonging and difference

To be human is to be rooted in a particular time and place and therefore to be different from most other people. The principal differences are to do with age, class, culture, disability, ethnicity, gender, language, nation, race, religion, sexuality and status. They are expressed through different perceptions, narratives, interests, standpoints and customs. Every individual belongs to a range of different groups, and therefore has a range of different belongings. Also, and partly in consequence, all individuals change and develop over time, as do all cultures, groups and communities.

In all subjects, the texts, visual material and electronic resources can reflect the reality that there are many different ways of being human and that cultural identities are continually developing. Similarly the tasks, problems and assignments that are set can reflect these aspects of the real world. In many subjects, there are also direct opportunities for teaching and learning about cultural differences, and differences of perception, interpretation, interest and narrative.

Globalisation and the global village

Countries, cultures and communities are not cut off from each other. On the contrary, there has been much borrowing, mingling and mutual influence over the centuries between different countries and cultural traditions. Events and trends in one place in the modern world are frequently affected by events and trends elsewhere. You cannot understand your own local world close at hand without seeing it as part of a global system. The global system has a range of interacting sub-systems: ecological, cultural, economic and political. There are benefits, but also dangers and difficulties.

Economic interdependence is an essential concept in geography. Ecological interdependence is fundamental in biology, chemistry and physics. Political interdependence is central in all studies of causation in history. Cultural interdependence, involving fusion, cross-over and mutual influences and borrowing, is a recurring feature in art, design, drama, literature, music and technology.

Learning from other places and times

Examples of high achievement are to be found in a wide range cultures, societies and traditions and not only in 'the west' or in modern times. They are the work of both women and men, of gay people as well as straight, and of disabled people as well as non-disabled. They are to be found in all areas of human endeavour – the arts and sciences, law and ethics, personal and family life, religion and spirituality, moral and physical courage, invention, politics, imagination.

In every subject, examples of achievement, invention, creativity, insight and heroism can be taken from a wide range of cultures, both in the present and the past.

Conflict resolution and justice

In all societies and situations – including families, schools, villages, nations, the world – there are disagreements and conflicts of interest. In consequence there is a never-ending need to construct, and to keep in good repair, non-violent ways of dealing with conflict – rules, laws, customs and systems that all people accept as reasonable and fair.

It is particularly in history, PSHEE and citizenship education that social and political concepts to do with conflict resolution and justice are taught and developed directly. Indirectly, they can be a dimension in all subjects, particularly literature and stories and the creative and performing arts.

Open and closed minds

All advances of knowledge and substantial achievements require a readiness to review and examine assumptions, expectations and perceptions that may be false or distorted. Such assumptions may be about the inherent superiority of one's own country, culture or ethnicity; the inherent superiority of either women or men; sexuality; disability; people of one's own generation; or the period of history in which one happens to live. The avoidance of stereotypes and unexamined beliefs, accompanied by keeping one's mind open to new information, evidence and points of view, is a constant struggle.

It is particularly in history, PSHEE and citizenship education that social and political concepts to do with prejudice and open-mindedness are taught and developed directly. Indirectly, they can be a dimension in all subjects, particularly literature and stories and the creative and performing arts. In science, technology and mathematics there is constant emphasis on attention to hard evidence and on the rigorous testing of hypotheses.

Open and closed views of 'us' and 'them are illustrated in the table below.

Views of us and them

Points of contrast	Closed views	Open views
Uniformity/diversity	They are all much the same	There is great diversity amongst them
Difference/similarity	They are significantly different from us	There are many commonalities between them and us
Inferiority/equality	They are morally and culturally inferior to us	There is both good and bad everywhere – both in them and us
Threat/trust	They are a threat to us	There are both real and perceived threats on both sides
Conflict/cooperation	There is no possibility of them and us living and working cooperatively together.	It is both possible and urgent that they and we should work together on solving or managing shared problems and on building mutual confidence

Talking and acting to learn

Introductory notes

How we teach, it has been said, is what we teach – the message is in the methodology teachers use as well as in the content they present. It is paradoxical and difficult, it follows, to teach about issues of equality and human dignity if these values are not reflected in how classrooms are organised.

Pupils should be able to participate in their learning and arrive at positions that may be different from those of their teachers. This can be achieved by organising discussions and enquiries in small groups. The forms of talk in groups that are most effective for learning are exploratory in nature and make higher order demands on those taking part. They involve pupils asking questions that require other pupils to offer opinions, make hypotheses, give reasons and reflect, and all members of a group working to create a shared understanding.

A frequent problem when running discussions in educational settings is that pupils go off-task – they chat rather than converse. Or else the discussion becomes over-heated or, as the term might be, under-heated – desultory, bored, disengaged, not going anywhere. There are suggestions on the following pages on how to manage such problems.

General points

Some tips for running purposeful discussions are outlined below. But first, some general points. It is almost always valuable to provide or organise:

■ opportunities to activate prior knowledge

■ explicit teaching of courtesies and conventions for speaking and listening

■ explicit teaching about how to work cooperatively with others

■ ensuring there are roles and tasks for everyone, and that everyone can adopt different roles at different times

■ explanation that different people have different ways of contributing – some are extraverts ('I do not know what I think till I hear what I say') whilst others like to compose their thoughts before they speak

■ opportunities for reflection and reporting back

■ groupings that combine pupils with difference learning styles, experiences, backgrounds and degrees of knowledge

■ awareness there may be gender differences in the ways girls and boys contribute to discussions, and in the ways they respond to competition and cooperation

■ opportunities to share opinions with the world beyond the classroom – for example in the rest of the school, displays in the local neighbourhood, letters to the local press, messages on 'have your say' sections of newspaper websites, blogs and social networking sites, and letters to local or national elected representatives.

Reflections – 34

Co-operative effort

When children bring language to bear on a problem within a small group their talk is often tentative, discursive, implicit and uncertain of direction...In an atmosphere of tolerance, of hesitant formulation and of co-operative effort the children can stretch their language to accommodate their own second thoughts, and the opinions of others. They can float their notions without having them dismissed.

– Bullock Report, 1975

Reflections – 35

Together

'We started a new project today, Mum,' announced 10-year-old Kate. 'What's it about?' asked her mother. 'The world,' came the reply. Then, noticing a look of surprise or dismay on her mother's face, Kate added: 'Don't worry it could be too difficult, Mum. There are two of us doing it together.'

– source unknown, 1970s

Everyday language and curriculum language

Types of difference	EVERYDAY LANGUAGE	CURRICULUM LANGUAGE
Mode	Mainly spoken	Mainly written
Reason for using language	To maintain or develop a relationship with a friend or peer	To demonstrate knowledge to a teacher or examiner
Relationships with others	Very or extremely important	Of little or no importance
Sense of personal identity and family background	Very or extremely important	Of little or no importance
Feelings – pleasure, annoyance, anxiety, etc	Expression of feelings is very common	Expression of personal feelings is not encouraged and is rare
Subject-matter	Of immediate and personal interest	Seldom of immediate interest
Location of subject-matter	Often can be seen as the talk takes place	Seldom can be seen as the writing takes place
Whether about shared experience	Often about an experience that the speaker and listener share	Seldom about an experience that the writer and reader share
Possibility and speed of feedback	Immediate feedback is provided on how well one is communicating	In the case of written language, feedback is not immediate, and may take hours, days or weeks
Non-verbal signs – facial expression, posture, gesture, etc	Extremely and unavoidably important	Of no importance at all
Jokes and humour	Frequent	Rare
Relationship between language and thought	Often you 'think aloud' – you discover your thoughts through the process of talking	You think first, then use language to express thought
Direction of communication	Forwards and backwards, with learning on both sides	One way
Lexical items	Mostly of one or two syllables, derived from Germanic or Anglo-Saxon sources	Many of two or three syllables, derived from Greek, Latin or French sources
Pronouns	Clear from the immediate situation what they refer to	Clarity depends on knowing and using grammatical rules
Technical terms	Seldom used	Must be used
Register of language	Frequent use of slang and colloquialisms	Formal language essential
Statements	Frequently short phrases, and not always in logical order	Must be complete sentences, with subject before verb
Grammar	Standard English not important and sometimes inappropriate	Standard English essential

Source: adapted slightly from Enriching Literacy, *Brent Language Service, 1998*

Everyday language and curriculum language

In collaborative work in small groups, there are opportunities for pupils to develop 'curriculum language', as distinct from 'everyday language'. The differences between these two different kinds of language are summarised opposite.

Another crucial distinction is to do with *cognitive challenge.*

If one bears in mind both sets of distinctions – curriculum/everyday and easy/challenging – four main types of language use can be identified in school classrooms They are referred to in the tabulation below with the terms 1) exercising 2) networking and nattering 3) talking to learn and 4) making the grade.

Traditionally, the way to get learners from the bottom left quartile ('networking and nattering') to top right ('making the grade') has been by way of the top left quartile ('exercising'). This has worked well for some learners, and continues to work well. It's often an appropriate route. But for some pupils, or even all pupils in some of the subjects they study, the route needs to take in the bottom right quartile ('talking to learn') – they need to engage in structured discussion with each other in pairs or small groups. For them, collaborative discussion is not a distraction from real work, or an optional extra; it is essential.

Getting started: one, two, four

It is often valuable to start by asking each individual to do, decide, write or choose something on their own. This gives them a secure base, so to speak, from which to go out and engage with others.

Then have them talk in pairs about what they have written or done. Then form fours or sixes, and share further.

All the classroom activities in Part 3 of this book can start with an introductory activity such as this. It is an excellent way of providing both security and challenge.

Objects to handle

It is often valuable for pupils to work with things that are tangible and which they can handle and arrange. Moving their hands seems to loosen their tongues and their minds.

For example, it is valuable to provide phrases, statements and quotations on separate slips of paper or cards, rather than on a single sheet of paper. This makes material literally as well as metaphorically easier to manage and gives pupils a sense of being in control. Also, of course, it is valuable to handle pictorial material (for example, most obviously, postcards and photographs) and three-dimensional objects.

All the classroom activities in Part 3 can include opportunities to handle and manipulate cards, visual material and objects.

Four types of language use in school classrooms

Register of English	Low level of cognitive challenge	High level of cognitive challenge
Curriculum language	**1. Exercising** Examples include giving rote-learned answers to questions, copying from books or the board, doing various sentence-completion exercises.	**4. Making the grade** Examples include writing answers in SATs and GCSE exams, and all or most written work in direct preparation for such tests and exams.
Everyday language	**2. Networking, nattering** Examples include text messages and postcards, and passing the time of day – chat about last night's TV, celebrities, sport, gossip.	**3. Talking to learn** Examples include talk within structured discussion exercises requiring genuine communication, and notes arising from such exercises.

Source: adapted slightly from Enriching Literacy, *Brent Language Service, 1998*

Jigsaw exercises

A jigsaw exercise typically has three stages:

1. Pupils form base groups – usually with three or else four members. They are given descriptions of the enquiry groups in which they will be working in the next stage and they decide amongst themselves who will go to which enquiry group. They go as representatives of their base group, with the responsibility of reporting back in the third stage.

2. Pupils work in enquiry groups, each enquiry group engaging in a different task.

3. They return to their base groups and report back on what they have done and learnt.

It is possible and valuable to organise a jigsaw exercise with nearly all the classroom activities in Part 3 of this book . One of the advantages of such exercises is that pupils are given responsibility for teaching each other.

Precise tasks

It is usually valuable to give precise unambiguous instructions about the actual outcome that one wants. 'Here are pictures of six people. Choose the two people you would most like to meet. For each of them write down the two questions you would most like to ask. You have ten minutes.'

Tight and clear instructions, leading to an obvious outcome in a fixed period of time, are liberating rather than cramping. Vague instructions ('discuss what you think of this') can merely dissipate energy and interest, and lead to much waste of time.

That said, it is sometimes valuable simply to say: 'Think aloud about this.'

All the classroom activities in Part 3 of this book can involve precise tasks.

Thought showers, and listing without discussing

This well-known activity also known as brainstorming can be invaluable. It involves a small group making a list without any discussion in the first instance. If it goes well, everyone feels able and willing to contribute, existing knowledge is activated and pooled, and an atmosphere of openness and mutual trust is established.

Listing without discussing does not come naturally. It can therefore be valuable and fun to practise it with non-serious material. For example: 'In one minute write down objects in this room.' Then: 'In a further minute write down things in this room that are unlikely to be on any other group's list.'

The next stage, when lists are made for a serious purpose, is to sort and prioritise the ideas that have been generated.

All the classroom activities in Part 3 of this book can involve the making of lists without discussion as part of the learning.

Reconstructing through talking

This is sometimes known as dictogloss and is an excellent way of introducing a key idea. It typically has three stages.

First, a short text is read aloud at normal speed. It could be an entry in an encyclopaedia, a book review, a passage in a textbook, a newspaper article or editorial, an extract from a guidebook, the abstract of an article and so on. The pupils listen without making notes.

Second, the same text is read aloud more slowly and this time pupils make notes of key words and phrases.

Third, pupils work in pairs or small groups, comparing their notes and trying to recreate the original text as fully and accurately as possible.

All the classroom activities in Part 3 of this book can involve the use of dictogloss.

Cloze procedure

This is another well-known activity that is invaluable for introducing a new piece of material.

Pupils are given a piece of text in which certain key words are blanked out. In pairs or groups, they try to guess what the missing word may be. When they have chosen a word to fill a gap, they can be asked to consult a thesaurus to find a better word, or to reassure themselves that the word they have chosen is indeed the most appropriate.

This develops sensitivity to nuances and gradations of meaning, and is a valuable stimulus to real discussion as different possibilities are compared and contrasted, and the final choice is chosen and justified.

All the activities in Part Two of this book can involve the use of cloze procedure.

Reconstituting

Take two different texts and cut them up into their separate sentences, and shuffle all the fragments together. In pairs or groups, pupils have to sort the fragments into two clusters and then to sequence them.

Or take ten (say) quotations, proverbs or sayings and cut each in half – again, the task is to re-constitute them.

Such exercises can be made considerably more demanding if the fragments are dealt out as in a game of cards, with each person having their own 'hand'. Each then has to read their hand to others, rather than merely show it.

All the classroom activities in Part 3 of this book can involve the reconstituting of a piece of text.

Committee games

It is frequently valuable to discuss material and ideas through a simulation exercise in which groups of pupils see themselves as a committee which has to choose between competing priorities. Typically, decisions have to be made about allocations of resources. It is sometimes possible to make the game real by providing some real money that has to be distributed.

Committee games can be made more demanding if they involve an element of role-playing, or if groups receive visits from lobbyists and applicants.

Several of the activities in Part 3 of this book can involve committee games.

Ground rules

Ask pupils to talk about what makes it difficult to contribute to a group discussion. They may come up with *other people dominating or stating their opinion forcefully, being ridiculed, being interrupted, feeling shy, feeling ignorant.* They then draw up a charter or set of rules for themselves. It may include references to *taking turns to speak, not making fun of others, not using put-downs, listening to others, not interrupting, trying to seek understanding rather than consensus.* The finally agreed ground rules can be put on the wall as a constant reminder.

Reflections – 36

Teaching about cultural diversity

There was once a pre-test, post-test experiment in relation to teaching about cultural diversity. The pre-test showed that the dominant view amongst the pupils was that foreigners are, as one child put it, stupid bastards. There followed some intensive teaching about high achievements in cultures different from the pupils' own. The post-test showed a marked shift had taken place in pupils' attitudes. This was expressed by one child with the statement that foreigners are cunning bastards.

– source unknown

Changing language

Words change in their meanings and implications over time, and mean different things to different people. Also, there are changing views over the decades of what is polite and what is offensive.

Reflections – 37

Don't point, Gregory

He attracted his mother's attention by yelling 'Look! She's black. Look, Mum, black woman.' – 'Don't point, Gregory. She's not black, she's coloured.' While from the other side of the road came shouting. Loud, uncouth and raucous. 'Golliwog, golliwog.' It was three young men. Holding up a wall they yelled through the funnel of their hands, ' Oi, sambo.'

– from Small Island *by Andrea Levy, set in London in the 1940s*

Changes of language occur partly because the outer world changes; partly because understandings of the world change; and partly because various groups and communities gain greater power and influence than hitherto so can insist that their voices and viewpoints are listened to and taken into account.

For example, the word 'black' used to be considered offensive and the word 'coloured' was considered polite. But in due course black people gained sufficient power to decide for themselves how they wished to be described, and the word 'coloured' became widely unacceptable.

Reflections – 38

Will not stand still

Words strain.
Crack and sometimes break, under the burden,
Under the tension, slip, slide, perish,
Decay with imprecision, will not stay in place,
Will not stay still.

– from Four Quartets *by T.S. Eliot*

Changes in language however do not necessarily lead to changes in attitudes or behaviour.

Reflections – 39

Nasty words

All the other children at my school are stupid. Except I'm not meant to call them stupid, even though this is what they are. I'm meant to say they have learning difficulties or that they have special needs. But this is stupid because everyone has learning difficulties because learning to speak French or understanding Relativity is difficult and also everyone has special needs...

But we have to use those words because people used to call children like the children at school spaz and crip and mong which were nasty words. But that is stupid too because sometimes the children from the school down the road see us in the street when we are getting off the bus and they shout, 'Special Needs! Special Needs!'

From The Curious Incident of the Dog in the Night Time *by Mark Haddon, 2003*

A further problem is that different words are used in different contexts. With regard to ethnicity, for example, there tend to be differences between:

- legal, administrative and official usage
- usage in most ordinary conversation amongst white people, reflected and reinforced by usage in the media
- usage reflecting the self-understanding of individuals and communities affected by racism
- usage in academia.

The terms 'race' (as in 'race relations' and 'race equality') and 'racial' ('racial group') occur widely in legal usage. They therefore often occur in official documents referring to legislation. Also, they often occur in everyday conversations and in the media. But nowadays they virtually never occur in academia, unless with inverted commas to signal they are problematic. The preferred term in academia is ethnicity. It is also the preferred term throughout this book.

It will be a long time before there is a shared vocabulary for talking and writing about race and ethnicity across all contexts even in the UK, let alone in the rest of the English-speaking world, or in international forums. Similarly, it will be a long time

Reflections – 40

Great vocabulary

I used to think I was poor. Then they told me I wasn't poor, I was needy. Then they told me it was self-defeating to think of myself as needy, I was deprived. Then they told me deprived had negative connotations, I was underprivileged. Then they told me underprivileged was overused, I was disadvantaged. Then they said disadvantage is a relative concept, not an absolute one. I still don't have a dime. But I sure have a great vocabulary.

(*Source unknown*)

before there is consensus around language in relation to disability, faith, gender and sexuality. There is a summary on the next page of some of the principal choices that have to be made. Later in this chapter there are notes on those choices.

A book such as this cannot stipulate how words relating to equalities should always be used. It can, however, be consistent in its own use of language. Also, it can and should contain an explanation of how and why it uses contested terms itself. Hence the notes that follow.

Equality/diversity

As moral and political values, these may be seen two sides of the same coin. Neither is complete without the other. But they can be current in different speech communities, with discourse of diversity being preferred by those who do not wish to talk about racism and unequal power relations. In UK and European law, the preferred term is equality. A phrase using both words (shortened to E & D) is in increasing use.

Race and ethnicity

Race appears in legislation, as for example in the terms *race equality*, *race relations* and *racial group*. There is no scientific basis for dividing the human species into races, however. The term *ethnicity*, which implies cultural, linguistic and religious aspects of identity as well as (sometimes but not always) visible differences, more accurately reflects the intentions in race relations legislation. Also, it is more consistent with the understanding that cultural racism (for example, Islamophobia and antisemitism) can be as serious as colour racism.

Disability/impairment/disablement

The Equality and Human Rights Commission advises that an impairment becomes a disability when adjustments are not provided to compensate for it: a person with an impairment is disabled by society's failure to provide an adjustment for it, not by the impairment itself. The term disablement is sometimes used to describe the processes which cause an impairment to become a disability.

What's in a word? – some of the choices

equality	diversity	
disability	impairment	
disabled people	people with disabilities	
gender	sex	
race	ethnicity	
racism	xenophobia	
BME people	ethnic minorities	
Gypsy	Traveller	Roma
Islamophobia	anti-Muslim racism	
faith	religion	belief
sensitivity	political correctness	

Gender/sex

The former term refers to social and cultural roles and expectations, the latter to biological differences. The original legislation in the UK refers to 'sex discrimination' but more recently the legal duty is to promote '*gender equality*'.

The term 'BME'

The term *BME* (short for 'black and minority ethnic') can be useful for providing a broad-brush overview in order to refer to all people not categorised as 'white British'. It is seldom if ever helpful, however, for clarifying the practical measures which need to be introduced to make improvements in provision. Further objections to the term include: it runs the risk of dehumanising, as does any such use of abbreviations (SEN, EAL, etc); it implies black people are not of a minority or minoritised background; it cannot be used grammatically as an adjective before a noun such as 'person' or 'people'; it reflects a simplistic majority/minority distinction that is frequently inaccurate or inappropriate; it is arguably no more than a code for 'coloured' or 'visibly different'. DCSF documentation on race equality increasingly does not use it.

The term 'Asian'

Publications sometimes use the term *Asian* as a blanket reference to Bangladeshi, Indian and Pakistani communities. However, these communities vary considerably in terms of social class and migration history; the impact on them of recent economic trends; the geographical area within Britain where they are mainly settled; religious tradition, culture and language; and the nature of the prejudice, hostility and discrimination they may encounter. There are few if any practical policies and measures that are relevant to all 'Asian' communities without exception.

Reflections – 41

What's happened?

Louis XVI: C'est une révolte?
A courtier: Non, Sire, c'est une révolution.

When the news arrived at Versailles of the Fall of the Bastille, July 1789

Reflections – 42

Guess what?

Back in the 1970s in a seminal study the sociologists Sally Hacker and Joseph Schneider asked 300 college students to select pictures from magazines and newspapers to illustrate different chapters in a sociology textbook. Half the students were given chapter headings like 'Social Man', 'Industrial Man' and 'Political Man'. The other half were given different but corresponding headings such as 'Society', 'Industrial Life' and 'Political Behaviour'. Guess what? The first group of students, from both sexes, consistently choose pictures with males only. The second group, working without 'man' selected images of both males and females.

– from The Language of Equality *by Ziauddin Sardar, 2008*

The term 'Black'

In an analogous way, publications sometimes use the blanket term *black*, without distinguishing between African and African-Caribbean communities. Occasionally, further, reports use the term *black* to refer to all people who may experience racism based on their physical appearance. Racism based on colour is a serious matter, most certainly. But the blanket term *black* can mask rather than clarify patterns of disadvantage and discrimination.

Islamophobia/anti-Muslim racism

The latter term is arguably clearer, since it does not imply a mental disorder. But the former is now current and is useful for referring to a general climate of opinion. Like antisemitism, it refers to a form of racism.

Religion/faith

Historically the former term has referred to a general tradition and to what academics sometimes call an ethno-religious identity, whereas the latter has referred to inner beliefs and commitments. Recently, this distinction has been changing, with 'faith' being used increasingly to refer to ethno-religious tradition rather than, necessarily, to inner beliefs.

Gypsy/Traveller

Not the same, since not all Gypsies are Travellers and not all Travellers are Gypsies. Usually best to use both, joined with 'and', not a slash.

Racism/xenophobia

Arguably the same, though also corresponding to visible/invisible differences, namely to differences of colour and culture respectively. The latter term is much more used in other European countries than in the UK.

Sensitivity/political correctness

The latter is usually a term of criticism, ridicule or abuse, and implies opposition, resistance or scepticism in relation to measures to promote greater equality, and to the need to use language sensitively and appropriately, as outlined in the notes above.

In so far as political correctness is a neutral term, as distinct from a loaded one, it refers, as mentioned above, to a concern for appropriate language. Being concerned about what is appropriate does not entail contending that certain words are always correct and others always wrong. It does, however, involve bearing in mind that certain words can give offence, even when no offence is intended; and that certain words and phrases seem to justify or be oblivious of, as distinct from challenge, patterns of unjust discrimination.

There are four concerns underlying the desire to review and revise terminology:

- Certain people have their rights, opportunities or freedoms restricted due to their categorisation as members of a group about which there are negative stereotypes.

- Such stereotypes are sometimes embodied in everyday language. If the language is changed the stereotypes may become weaker and it may be easier in consequence to challenge discrimination.

- If the labelling terminology is rendered problematic, people will be made to think consciously about how they describe someone.

- Once labelling is a conscious activity, the individual merits of a person, rather than their perceived membership of a group, will become more apparent.

Reflections – 43

Mists up the windows

I would try not to be shrill or earnest. An amused tolerance always comes over best, particularly on television. Paradox works well and mists up the windows, which is handy. 'The loss of liberty is the price we pay for freedom' type thing.

from The History Boys *by Alan Bennett, 2004*

Reflections – 44

Flying to the dictionary

'Are you in love with him?'
'I don't much care for that word,' she said.
'Why not?'
'Because I don't know what it means.'
He gave a quiet yell. 'Oh don't say that. It's a word you must have often come across in conversation and literature. Are you going to tell me it sends you flying to the dictionary each time?'

– *from* Lucky Jim *by Kingsley Amis, 1954*

The two teachers

One day, a teacher working at Selfbury School got a new job at Otherham School. During the holiday before taking up her new post she happened to meet Mullah Nasruddin, who mentioned he knew Otherham School. 'What's it like there?' she asked.

'Well,' said Mullah Nasruddin. 'What's it like at Selfbury School?'

'Terrible,' said the teacher. 'The head's a little Hitler, the children are savages, my colleagues were for ever stabbing me in the back and the local authority officers and advisers were a pack of lifeless grey suits. But anyway, what's it like at Otherham?'

'I'm sorry to have to tell you,' said Mullah Nasruddin, 'that you'll find the school you are going to is very similar to the school you are coming from'. The teacher went on her way lamenting. The next stage of her career would consist of one battle and defeat after another.

During that same school holiday there was another teacher moving from Selfbury School to Otherham. She too happened to meet Mullah Nasruddin. 'What's it like at Otherham?' she asked. ''Well,' he said. 'What's it like at Selfbury?'

'Wonderful.' said the teacher. 'The head was always supportive, the children were keen to learn, my colleagues couldn't be more helpful. I'm really sorry to be leaving, I can tell you. But anyway, what's it like at Otherham?'

'I'm pleased to be able to tell you,' said Mullah Nasruddin, 'that you'll find the school you are going to is very similar to the school you are coming from'. The teacher went on her way rejoicing. The next stage of her life would consist of one fruitful encounter and exchange after another.

Source: traditional

PART 3

Subjects and skills: aspects of curriculum content

Art, craft and design

Importance

Art, craft and design are important for teaching and learning about equalities, difference and cohesion because they enable children to:

- gain a lively sense of aspirations, needs, problems and desires that all human beings have in common
- learn to appreciate and value the specific and distinctive nature of images and artefacts across times and cultures, and to understand the contexts in which they were made
- develop confidence, competence, imagination, self-management and creativity in expressing their own identities
- reflect critically on their own and other people's work, judging quality, value and meaning
- take risks and learn from their mistakes
- appreciate the role that art, craft and design play in the creative and cultural industries that enrich and shape the lives of people, and influence the views they have of themselves and others.

Key concepts

Key concepts in the study of art, craft and design include creativity, originality, competence, understanding of cultural contexts, criticism, appreciation and evaluation.

Key processes

Key processes and skills include:

- developing ideas and intentions by working from first-hand observation, experience, inspiration and imagination, and from sketchbooks, journals, photographs and video clips
- expressing and visualising perception and invention, and feelings, experiences and ideas
- using a wide range of materials, tools, drawing techniques, codes, symbols and conventions
- appreciating how codes and conventions are used to convey ideas and meanings in and between different cultures and contexts
- reflecting on and evaluating one's own and others' work, adapting and refining images and artefacts at all stages of the creative process
- interpreting and negotiating design briefs and specifications, and discussing and amending drafts
- analysing, selecting and questioning critically, and making reasoned choices when developing personal work
- exploring, studying and using media, processes and techniques in 2D, 3D and new technologies, and both fine art and applied art practices.

Reflections – 46

No mystery

Steven Connolly, aged 15, visits Sheba, an art teacher.

There was a book of Degas reproductions lying on her desk – she had brought it in, hoping to charm her Year Eight girls with ballerinas and when Connolly picked it up, she encouraged him to look inside.

He began leafing through the book, stopping every now and then to let Sheba paraphrase the commentary on a particular painting or sculpture. She was very pleased with his response to a painting entitled Sulking. Reading from the book, she informed him that the relationship between the man and the woman in the picture was mysterious and that nobody knew for sure which one of them was meant to be the sulker.

After looking at the picture again Connolly declared that there was no mystery – the man was clearly the sulking party. The woman was bending towards him, trying to get something from him, and his hunched, irascible posture indicated his displeasure. Sheba was impressed by this analysis and she congratulated Connolly on being an acute observer of body language. After he had gone she found herself chuckling aloud. Connolly's Special Needs teacher would have been very shocked, she thought, if he could have seen his learning disabled pupil chattering so enthusiastically about Degas!

– from Notes on a Scandal *by Zoe Heller, 2003*

Reflections – 47

The experience was liberating

My work is a painting from a photograph the day I shaved my head. The style I chose to paint in was inspired by Jenny Saville's more recent work. The expression on my face is literally my initial reaction to how this experience made me feel. Before I shaved my head, my hair was so much part of my image: it was long and bleached blond. My hair made me feel attractive and it was the most prominent part of my image. This piece explores the emotions I experienced when I chose to remove the part of my appearance that I felt so strongly connected to. The question my piece poses is how strongly image is connected to identity and how it feels to remove that part of yourself. Though I felt as though I had removed my femininity, the experience was liberating.

– Lydia Burchill, 2006

Reflections – 48

Smug, complacent, delusional

... I have been married for 15 years and I think things have gone pretty well. We have four perfectly acceptable children, we all get along OK, and as husbands go, I'm not a bad lot ... My wife stays at home to look after the children because returning to the teaching job she loved was made impossible by the incompatibility of teacher's pay and the cost of childcare... She loves it, doesn't she? Well, that's what I had assumed, until an incident a couple of weeks ago that shocked my smug, complacent, delusional self to the core...

The paintings of Louise Bourgeois are so filled with rage, fear and frustration that, for the first time in my life, I began to understand what it must be like to be a woman. To have to accept that the world's view is male and all the assumptions that come with it, such as: everything you do and say is seen and judged through the prism of your sexuality, that the expectation is you will fulfil the multiple roles of mother, housekeeper, companion, worker and lover with deference and gratitude, and that men – lazy, selfish, conceited men – are not forced to wear the same, or any other straitjacket.

– Will Gompertz, 2007

Classroom activities

Everyday life

Pupils compare and contrast depictions of everyday life in Egyptian wall paintings, Greek vases, the Bayeux Tapestry, Indian miniatures, Japanese and Chinese art, Breughel the Elder, modern photography, advertisements, family snapshots and archive photographs. They create images of their own daily life and of life in their community and neighbourhood, using some of the same methods and approaches.

Who, what and where are we?

Pupils answer various kinds of questionnaire about their personal interests, and in this way reflect on their own identities, cultural roots and personal qualities, and their experiences of belonging and exclusion. They then administer the same or similar questionnaires to others as part of a survey, and present their findings and personal thoughts through collages, artefacts, installations, e-zines, video diaries, powerpoint or interactive web pages.

Posters

Pupils examine and discuss a collection of posters and publicity material on themes such as sustainable development, equal opportunities, respect for people who are disabled, combating homophobia, racial justice and human rights. They establish criteria for evaluation of such posters with regard to colour, composition, shape, font and format in the lettering register of language, and images and assumptions relating to people and situations. They then design and create their own posters and display these in public spaces within their school and the local neighbourhood.

Fusion

Pupils study the principal international influences on artists whose work is currently on show at a local gallery and the ways their work represents fusion of a range of traditions, cultures and genres. They then create their own work, similarly drawing on a range of genres and traditions.

Puppets

Pupils examine with care, curiosity and respect stick puppets from India, Indonesia and Thailand, and design, make and use their own. Instead or as well, they design and make shadow puppets and theatres.

Citizenship

Importance

Citizenship education is important for teaching and learning about equalities, difference and cohesion because it enables children to:

- acquire the knowledge, skills and understanding to play an effective role in public life, both now and in the future

- engage in discussion, debate. decision-making and advocacy in relation to topical and controversial issues

- develop respect for a range of different national, religious and ethnic identities

- understand how society has changed and is changing in the UK, Europe and the wider world

- engage and negotiate with opinions, values and ideas different from their own

- evaluate information, make informed judgments and reflect on the consequences of their actions now and in the future.

Key concepts

Key concepts in citizenship education include:

The rule of law – deliberative and representative democracy, the management and resolution of conflict, the tension between force and persuasion, the need for agreement on processes and procedures of debate and decision-making

Rights and responsibilities – including the rights of children and young people, the rights of disabled people, the rights of women, and rights relating to ethnicity, religion and culture; and fundamental freedoms, including freedom of speech and its limits

Pressure – the activities and influence of lobbying and campaigning organisations, and ways and conventions for approaching one's own elected representatives

Identity and belonging – the need to balance local, national and supra-national loyalties; the concept of global or cosmopolitan citizenship

Interdependence and globalisation – and the need for international and intercultural cooperation

---

Reflections – 49

Keep these distinctions clearly in mind

The Scots (originally Irish, but by now Scotch) were at this time inhabiting Ireland, having driven the Irish (Picts) out of Scotland; while the Picts (originally Scots) were now Irish (living in brackets) and *vice versa*. It is essential to keep these distinctions clearly in mind (and *verce visa*).

– from 1066 And All That *by W.C.Sellar and R.J.Yeatman, 1931*

Reflections – 50

Guiding principles

It is the year 3136. A starship is on its way from earth to colonise a distant planet. Despite advances in astrophysics and space technology, the journey will take several generations of earth time. To prevent ageing, the passengers are put into a kind of hibernation. They can think but all have totally forgotten, for the duration of the journey, their name, gender, ethnicity, class, status, income, age, level of intelligence, health and fitness, personality traits, religion, political attitudes, and physical attractiveness.

No one knows, for example, whether they will be in a minority group in certain respects, or the majority. Nor does anyone know whether most other people will be cleverer or stronger than themselves, or whether on the contrary they will be amongst the brightest, healthiest, most energetic and most capable.

The condition of space hibernation means that everyone is in a cocoon, and cannot even debate with others, let alone form coalitions and majorities. They can, however, all think.

You are a passenger on the starship and you spend your time wondering what kind of society you will wish to help establish when the starship eventually arrives at its destination. What in your view should the guiding principles for the new society be? What rights will all members of the society have? What responsibilities?

Think about care of children; education; law and order; gender equality; disability; sexuality; ethnicity, religion and culture; personal freedoms; decision-making.

– from an idea by Brian Wren, drawing on A Theory of Justice *by John Rawls*

Key processes

Key skills and processes in citizenship education include:

- engaging critically but appreciatively with a range of different ideas, opinions, beliefs and values when exploring topical, emotive and controversial issues

- researching, planning and undertaking enquiries into issues and problems, using a range of information, sources and research techniques

- engaging in advocacy, lobbying and representation through a range of activities, including discussion groups, formal debates, letters and emails, websites, and music, art, theatre and literature

- understanding and explaining sympathetically views, opinions, narratives which one disagrees with or finds unsettling

- using and interpreting a range of media and ICT both as sources of information and as ways of expressing and communicating ideas

Classroom activities

Have your say

Pupils study differing accounts of the same event, for example the differences between a report on the website of BBC News and reports in various tabloids. What is fact and what is fiction? What language is used? Is there an attempt to present balanced arguments? Are ideas presented as clear-cut, or can you see that even people directly involved are uncertain? Whose voice do you hear through the report? Does the report tell you what to think, or are you presented with evidence that helps you make up your own mind? Does the report reinforce readers' prejudices, or does it challenge them? If the report is recent, pupils send their own comments to the editor, or else submit them to the paper's *Have Your Say* section on its website.

Supporting and assisting people in need

Pupils are given, or they themselves raise, a sum of money. Alternatively, they use imaginary money. They are also given descriptions of a range of charitable projects and decide how to allocate their real or imaginary money between them. More elaborately, they can role-play the discussions, with different individuals or groups taking on different advocacy roles. Instead or as well, they make visits to, or receive visits from, real projects.

Looking ahead

Pupils look at a selection of today's national newspapers, either the print editions or those online, or this week's local papers; or at the most recently published statement of the central government's legislative intentions (the Queen's Speech); or at the legislative intentions of the Scottish Parliament or Welsh Assembly. They discuss these and decide which of the issues they would like to influence, if they possibly can. They learn how to write letters, faxes or email messages to their own elected representatives; send various messages; and keep a record of the answers they receive.

Not easy being British

Working in small groups, pupils answer questions of the kind that are asked in citizenship tests. How relevant do they consider the questions to be? If a question appears irrelevant can they nevertheless guess why it was asked? What suggestions do they have for questions that are more relevant? More specifically, can they come up with questions which are more appropriate for people such as themselves? They go on to discuss concepts of Britishness and national identity and to compare their own views with those of others.

Equal opps

In simulation or reality, pupils are involved in the appointment of a new member of staff at their school. They devise a job description and person specification and use these when shortlisting; they then draw up a set of questions to be asked at interview, and procedures to be adopted; they conduct the interviews and after their decision give feedback to the candidates who were unsuccessful. Throughout the process they are mindful of good practice in relation to legislation regarding age, disability, ethnicity, faith, gender and sexuality.

Design and technology

Importance

Design and technology is important for teaching and learning about equalities, difference and cohesion because it enables children to:

- combine practical and technological skills with creative thinking to design and make products and systems that meet human needs

- learn to use current technologies and consider the impact of future technological developments

- learn to think creatively and intervene to improve the quality of life, solving problems as individuals and members of a team

- identify needs and opportunities and respond with ideas, products and systems, challenging expectations where appropriate

- combine practical and intellectual skills with an understanding of aesthetic, technical, cultural, health, social, emotional, economic, industrial and environmental issues. As they do so, they evaluate present and past design and technology, and its uses and effects.

Key concepts

Key concepts in design and technology include:

- *Designing and making*, and understanding that these have aesthetic, environmental, technical, economic, ethical and social dimensions and impacts on the world

- *Cultural understanding*, for example appreciation of how products evolve according to users' and designers' needs, beliefs, ethics and values and how they are influenced by local customs and traditions and available materials

- *Creativity* – making links between principles of good design, existing solutions and technological knowledge to develop innovative products and processes

- *Critical evaluation* – analysing existing products and solutions to inform designing and making.

Key processes

Key processes in design and technology include:

- generating, developing, modelling and communicating ideas in a range of ways, using appropriate strategies

- responding creatively to briefs, developing one's own proposals and producing specifications for products

- planning and organising activities, and then shaping, forming, mixing, assembling and finishing materials, components and ingredients

- assessing which hand and machine tools, equipment and computer-aided design and manufacture (CAD/CAM) facilities are the most appropriate in order to solve technical problems.

Reflections – 51

Technologist and technician

The immense social significance of the distinction between the terms technologist and technician cannot be over-emphasised. The term 'technician' came to cover the full range of people who ... made things work and continued to make them work. But their status was inferior; they worked to the orders of their patrons, clients, employers or managers, who were not required to have any of the requisite practical technical knowledge or capability. The establishment of the role of professional technologist such as engineers, architects, town planners and financiers reinforced rather than diminished this distinction. In their training and in their professional work there was no need for them to lay bricks or saw timber.

... Technology education in the National Curriculum marks an attempt to override such old distinctions and especially to break out of the low status of technical education and to bring technological education from higher education into the schools. It is also an attempt to demonstrate that technology is an appropriate and important subject for the education of all children, including the most able.

– John Eggleston, 2001

Reflections – 52

Historically

Historically ... males were associated with what is technical and females with what is not technical. This emerged from the basic divide that associated femininity with nurturing, connection and the body, and masculinity with objectivity, separation and the mind.

The notion of the living female universe to be nurtured and protected emerged in Greek and early pagan philosophies. The challenge to this perspective, the right of man to have dominion over the earth, came into ascendancy in the 18th and 19th centuries as the tensions between social conventions and technological development grew. The emerging discourse surrounding technology placed aesthetics in opposition to the technical, and the inventor, the user, the thinker about and reactor to technology was male ...Men could invent machines, and women and children could operate them ... Consequently, technical competence was seen as integral to masculinities and women were positioned as technically incompetent. In schools, these practices were reflected in the separation of craft, design and technology, which boys studied, from home economics, which girls studied.

Patricia Murphy, 2007

Classroom examples

Playground

Pupils devise and administer a questionnaire about fellow-pupils' likes and dislikes about the school playground and other public spaces. They propose improvements that could be made and make models or plans to illustrate their proposals.

Buffet meal

Pupils design and make an informal buffet for a group of people from a range of religious and cultural backgrounds. They need therefore to research the various cultures to establish probable likes and dislikes and unacceptable foods.

Clothing

Pupils create a display of clothing from different parts of the world and provide labels explaining the technology used to manufacture them from raw material to finished product. As appropriate, they comment also on religious and cultural factors.

Intermediate technology

Pupils visit the websites of voluntary organisations concerned with promoting intermediate and appropriate technology, and design and create web pages to summarise their views. They design and make a folding structure capable of supporting material for a temporary shelter at a time of a natural or humanitarian disaster, in the UK or elsewhere.

Sustainable development

Taking ideas from the pack *Live well, live wisely* published by the Intermediate Technology Development Group pupils study the concept of sustainability throughout the world; research recycling and waste collection activities in their own locality; and compare and contrast projects in their local neighbourhood with projects elsewhere. They then design and model a waste collection point that could be set up in their own school, and an awareness-raising and publicity campaign to encourage other pupils – and all staff – to use it.

As part of the project they evaluate various products in use at their school, considering questions such as the following. What raw materials were used to make the product? How and where were the raw materials extracted and processed? How was the product manufactured? How was it transported to a market? How is it advertised? How is it reused or disposed of after its first use? How is the packaging reused or disposed of?

English

Importance

English language and literature are important for teaching and learning about equalities, difference and cohesion because they enable children to:

- develop the skills in speaking, listening, reading and writing that are needed for participation in the cultural, political and economic life of their society

- become enthusiastic and critical readers of stories, poetry and drama , as also of non-fiction and media texts

- gain a lively sense of aspirations, needs, problems and desires that all human beings have in common

- develop confidence, competence, imagination, self-management and creativity in expressing their own identities

- take risks and learn from their mistakes

- appreciate the power of language to shape perceptions, particularly in contexts of inequality and unfair discrimination

- appreciate the role that language plays in the creative and cultural industries that enrich and shape their lives, and influence the views they have of themselves and others.

Key concepts

Key concepts include competence in communication and comprehension, and in adopting conventions required in different genres and for different audiences and contexts; creativity, and seeing and making fresh connections, and using conventions in new and surprising ways; cultural understanding, including appreciation of how spoken and written language evolve in response to social and technological change and relate to identity and cultural diversity; critical understanding, including the formation of independent views through the use of logic, evidence and reasoned argument.

Key processes

Key processes and skills in English include:

- speaking fluently, adapting talk to a wide range of familiar and unfamiliar contexts and purposes, including those requiring confident and fluent use of standard English

---

Reflections – 53

The origins of speech

He teaches Communications 101: Communication Skills and Communications 201: Advanced Communication Skills. Although he devotes hours of each day to his new discipline, he finds its first premise, as enunciated in the Communications 101 handbook, preposterous. 'Human society has created language in order that we may communicate our thoughts, feelings and intentions to each other.' His own opinion, which he does not air, is that the origins of speech lie in song, and the origins of song in the need to fill out with sound the overlarge and rather empty human soul.

– from Disgrace *by J.M.Coetzee, 2000*

Reflections – 54

Betrayed and brutalised

We have so betrayed and brutalised language that we have forgotten that ... it is ... sacred, ... a gift at some immemorial time mysteriously bestowed. Even the behaviourists are beginning to question their own theory that language is a simple human function that has evolved, over millenniums, from the grunting of bears and apes.

We have lost our respect for this given treasure and now care so little to foster its growth that we have all become like Humpty-Dumpty: 'When I use a word,' he says in *Alice through the Looking Glass*, 'it means exactly what I mean it to mean'. This is all very well, perhaps, for somebody who is living down a rabbit hole, but not for us, if we are truly to understand each other and try to communicate ideas; we have to admit that words exist in their own right, that they have antecedents, long family trees, and are not just foundlings left on a doorstep for anybody to pick up and do with as they will. If I were a hero the maiden I would set out to rescue would be language.

from The World of the Hero *by P.L.Travers, 1989*

- presenting information clearly and persuasively to others, selecting the most appropriate way to structure and organise their speech for clarity and effect

- selecting from strategies to adapt speaking and listening flexibly in different circumstances

- reflecting and commenting critically on their own and others' performances

- listening to complex information and responding critically, constructively and cogently in order to clarify points and challenge ideas

- judging the intentions, standpoint and bias of a speaker or author

- working purposefully in groups, negotiating and building on the contributions of others to complete tasks or reach consensus

- using a range of dramatic approaches to explore complex ideas, texts and issues in scripted and improvised work

- engaging both with the English literary heritage and with contemporary writers, and with writers throughout the English-speaking world.

Classroom examples

Journeys

Using a resource such as *The Journey* by Marcia Hutchinson, pupils conduct interviews with people who took part in a major journey (from another country to UK, or from one part of UK to another) in their youth and construct pieces of prose which tell their stories. They include expectations before the journey began; things that happened on the way; initial feelings on arrival; and tasks of settling down and developing a sense of belonging.

Identity and struggle

Pupils read and study the stories for teenagers in *Walking a Tightrope* edited by Rehana Ahmed and comment in various genres of writing, and in various oral styles, on character, setting and mood; author perspective and voice; significant detail; starting and finishing; and creativity in language and narrative. They then write similar stories themselves.

Book festival

Using the collections from booksellers about disability, homophobia, antiracism or cultural diversity, or of books especially likely to be of interest to boys, pupils write reviews and give talks; write to the authors; and take part in a mini literature festival at which awards are made to the books considered best.

The best words in the best order

Pupils role-play the drafting sub-committee which (it is imagined) produced the final version of the Magna Carta, to which King John agreed on 15 June 1215. The basis for their deliberations is a draft created by two of their members. This could be a literal translation (http://www.constitution.org/eng/magnacar.htm), or else in age-appropriate modern English. The committee is chaired by Archbishop Stephen Langton and the two members defending their draft are Peter Fitz Herbert and Hubert De Burgh. Also present are Jocelyn of Bath and Glastonbury, who is a devout Christian; Hugh of Lincoln, a socialist; Alan of Galloway, a nit-picking pedant; and Philip d'Aubigny, who is bitterly opposed to political correctness.

See and hear ME

Pupils read, study and perform the poem which starts 'What do you see, nurses, what do you see?' and from which there is an extract on page 3 of this book in *Reflections – 6*. They then write similar poems themselves, exploring and expressing the inner feelings, worries, memories and desires of people who are too often voiceless, ignored and invisible.

Challenging the media

Pupils view extracts from *Islamophobia* and from *Safe Place: combating racist myths against asylum seekers*, both produced by Show Racism the Red Card, and then engage in activities which aim to develop empathy with people seeking asylum, and which are about distorted media coverage of Muslims and Islam. In addition, they watch sections of the *Faces of the World* DVD, produced by Save the Children, similarly about media distortions. They express their responses through real or imagined letters to the local or national press or to councillors or MPs; or through exhibitions and street theatre in their school or the local neighbourhood.

Geography

Importance

Geography is important for teaching and learning about equalities, difference and cohesion because it enables children to:

- understand where places are, how places and landscapes are formed, how people and their environment interact, and how a diverse range of economies, societies and environments are interconnected. It builds on pupils' own experiences to investigate places at all scales, from the personal to the global

- engage in questioning, investigation and critical thinking about issues affecting the world and people's lives, now and in the future

- see themselves as global citizens by exploring their own place in the world, their values and their responsibilities to other people, to the environment and to the sustainability of the planet

- develop understanding of concepts such as globalisation, world society, interdependence, sustainable development and spaceship earth

- reflect on ways in which personal, cultural and national identity is bound up with perceptions of, and feelings about, natural landscape and public spaces

- are helped to know their immediate environment and neighbourhood better and to see their locality within the wider context of regional, national and international affairs

---

Reflections – 55

Did not even know

Geography had been one of his strong points. He was aware of the rivers of Asia in their order, and of the principal products of Uruguay; and he could name the capitals of nearly all the United States.

But he had not been instructed for five minutes in the geography of his native country, of which he knew neither the boundaries nor the rivers nor the terrene characteristics. He could have drawn a map of the Orinoco, but he could not have found the Trent in a day's march; he did not even know where his drinking water came from.

– from Clayhanger *by Arnold Bennett, set in 1872*

Key concepts

Key concepts in geography include:

Place – understanding the physical and human characteristics of real places

Space – understanding the interactions between places and the networks created by flows of information, people and goods, knowing where places and landscapes are located, why they are there, the patterns and distributions they create, how and why these are changing and the implications for people

Scale – appreciating different scales – from personal and local to national, international and global, and making links between scales to develop understanding of geographical ideas

Interdependence – exploring the social, economic, environmental and political connections between places, and understanding the significance of interdependence in change, at all scales

Physical and human processes – understanding how sequences of events and activities in the physical and human worlds lead to change in places, landscapes and societies

Environmental interaction and sustainable development – understanding that the physical and human dimensions of the environment are interrelated and together influence environmental change

Cultural understanding and diversity – appreciating the differences and similarities between people, places, environments and cultures, and how people's values and attitudes differ and influence social, environmental, economic and political issues.

Key processes

Key processes and skills in geography include:

- asking geographical questions, thinking critically, constructively and creatively

- collecting, recording and displaying information

- identifying bias, opinion and abuse of evidence in sources when investigating social issues

Reflections – 56

Beyond their world

Beyond their garden in summer were fields of wheat and barley and oats, which sighed and rustled and filled the air with sleepy pollen and earth scents. These fields were large and flat, and stretched away to a distant line of trees set in the hedgerows.

To the children at that time these trees marked the boundary of their world.

Beyond their world enclosed by the trees there was, they were told, a wider world, with other hamlets and villages and towns and the sea and, beyond that, other countries, where people spoke languages different from their own. Their father had told them so.

But they had no mental picture of these, they were but ideas, unrealised: whereas in their own little world within the tree boundary everything appeared to them more than life-size, and more richly coloured.

– from Lark Rise to Candleford *by Flora Thompson, set in an English village in the 1880s*

- finding creative ways of using and applying geographical skills and understanding to create new interpretations of place and space

- selecting and using fieldwork tools and techniques appropriately, safely and efficiently

- using atlases, globes, maps at a range of scales, photographs, satellite images and other geographical data

- constructing maps and plans at a variety of scales, using graphical techniques to present evidence.

Classroom activities

Guided walk of local neighbourhood

Using *Global Reading*, published by Reading International Solidarity Centre (details and a quiz at www.risc.org.uk/introgame.html) pupils consider their immediate neighbourhood and ask: Where does this road lead to? Where did the stone for this building come from? How did the person who built this house make their money? Why is this street named after a

place in India? Where do goods in the shops come from? After further research, some of it requiring digital photography, they add information on outline maps of the area and produce a world map display, highlighting the places to which their area is linked. They build up their local-global map, adding appropriate symbols and a key. They then develop a guided walk with activities at each stage to introduce the variety of ways in which the area is linked to the rest of the world.

Geoblogs

Pupils create blogs which look at news stories within a geographical perspective. Possible topics include natural disasters and their impacts around the world, the concept of global footprint, fair trade, sustainable development, refugees. Or they may use World 66 to customise a map of the world for their own personal travels or the RGS Geography in the News website. Unlike a message board, which can be random, a geoblog must be organised in such a way that it is built up into a coherent pattern that becomes more complete, rather than more confusing, as it builds up.

Eco-schools

Pupils visit the websites of eco-schools around the world and draw up action plans for similar projects in their own school. Instead or as well, they role-play a committee which makes grants, visit the sites of winners throughout the world and decide which they consider best.

Behind the logo

Pupils investigate how the British public is implicated in exploitation of workers – usually females – in producing goods and services. (See, for example, *Looking behind the Logo* and *Trading Away Our Rights: women working in global supply chains*, both published by Oxfam.)

Grameen Project

Pupils investigate the work of the United Nations Development Fund for Women to support women's projects, and Fairtrade initiatives to support women to become self-sufficient. Within this context they examine the success of the Grameen Bank which was the 2006 winner of the Nobel Peace Prize, along with its founder Muhammed Yunus. Ninety-six per cent of the poorest people funded by Grameen Bank are women.

History

Importance

History is important for teaching and learning about equalities, difference and cohesion because it enables children to:

- have a sense of their own identity within historical narratives at personal, local, national and international levels

- ask and answer questions of the present by engaging with the past

- make connections within and across different periods and societies

- investigate Britain's relationships with the wider world

- develop a sense of the struggle over the centuries, within and between countries, to address inequalities and to promote justice.

Key concepts

Key concepts in the study of history include the following:

Chronological understanding – understanding and using appropriately dates, vocabulary and conventions that describe historical periods and the passing of time, and building a chronological framework of periods and using this to place new knowledge in its historical context.

Cultural, ethnic and religious diversity – understanding the diverse experiences and ideas, beliefs and attitudes of women, men and children in past societies, and of disabled people and members of cultural minorities, and of people in all social classes, and how these have shaped the world.

Change and continuity – identifying and explaining change and continuity within and across periods of history.

Cause and consequence – analysing and explaining the reasons for, and results of, historical events, situations, trends and changes.

Significance – considering the significance of events, people and developments in their historical context and in the present day.

Interpretation – understanding why historians and others have interpreted events, people and situations in different ways, and evaluating a range of interpretations of the past to assess their validity.

Reflections – 58

Cannot be interested

History, real solemn history, I cannot be interested in.... I read it a little as a duty; but it tells me nothing that does not either vex or weary me. The quarrels of popes and kings, with wars and pestilences in every page; the men all so good for nothing, and hardly any women at all – it is very tiresome.

– *from* Northanger Abbey *by Jane Austen, 1798*

Reflections – 59

Remained for her an English hero

At university, Martha had made friends with a Spanish girl, Cristina. The common history of their two countries lay centuries back, but even so, when Cristina had said, in a moment of friendly teasing, 'Francis Drake was a pirate', she had said 'No he wasn't', because she knew he was an English hero and a Sir and an Admiral and therefore a Gentleman ... Later, she looked up Drake in a British encyclopaedia, and while the word 'pirate' never appeared the words 'privateer' and 'plunder' frequently did, and she could quite see that one person's plundering privateer might be another person's pirate, but even so Sir Francis Drake remained for her an English hero, untainted by this knowledge.

– *from* England, England *by Julian Barnes, 1998*

Reflections – 57

Hot potato

While at school, I dropped history like a hot potato the very first chance I got because not only was I not reflected in it for 99 per cent of the subject, but when I was included, it was always in a negative light. Quite frankly, I hated history. I hope for a subject that is broader-based, with more depth, and from a few more perspectives, in its teaching today. To put it in a nutshell, I hope for a lot better for my daughter.

– *Malorie Blackman, 2007*

Key processes

Key processes and skills in history include:

- identifying and investigating, individually and as part of a team, specific historical questions or issues

- identifying, selecting and using a range of historical sources, including textual, visual and oral sources and artefacts, and evaluating these to reach well-argued and coherent conclusions

- using existing and emerging technologies where appropriate, and providing well-structured narratives, explanations and descriptions of the past

- understanding the major events, changes and developments in British, European and world history covering at least the medieval, early modern, industrial and twentieth century periods

- studying the development of trade, colonisation, industrialisation and technology, the British Empire and its impact on different people in Britain and overseas, pre-colonial civilisations, the nature and effects of the slave trade, and resistance and decolonisation

- studying the changing nature of conflict between countries and peoples and its lasting impact on national, ethnic, cultural or religious issues, including the impact of the two world wars and the Holocaust, and the role of European and international institutions in resolving conflicts

- using ICT to research information about the past, process historical data, and select, organise and present their findings

- make links between history and other subjects and areas of the curriculum, including citizenship.

Classroom activities

A merry tale

Pupils watch *The Adventures of Robin Hood*, starring Errol Flynn and Olivia de Haviland and/or *Robin Hood – Prince of Thieves* starring Kevin Costner. Also they read extracts from *The Merry Adventures of Robin Hood* by Howard Pyle (1883), plus more recent re-tellings of the legend. They then form two research teams, the one investigating what really happened in King John's reign and the other the mythical figure known as Robin Hood. With drama, fiction or video they present the story of Magna Carta, showing it's every bit as exciting as the legends of Robin Hood.

National identity

Pupils create and illustrate timelines showing relationships over the centuries between England, Ireland, Scotland and Wales, noting different perspectives and stories in the four nations at different times, and in different social classes, and the impact of urbanisation and the Empire. They investigate current views of British identity and of how it is changing.

Local neighbourhood and community

Pupils study ways in which their local area has changed over the course of time. They investigate education, houses and housing, migration and movement to the area from overseas and other parts of the UK; the building of factories; markets; religious observance; treatment of the poor and care of the sick; law and order; sport, leisure and the impact of national and international events and developments.

Timelines

Pupils create timelines such as the one on pages 89-91 of this book, showing the development of equalities legislation over the decades.

Reflections – 60

Never dead

The past is never dead. It's not even past.

– *William Faulkner,* Intruder in the Dust

Reflections – 61

They will teach you

They will teach you that a white man called Mungo Park discovered Niger River. That is rubbish. Our people fished in the Niger long before Mungo Park's grandfather was born. But in your exam, write it was Mungo Park,

– *from* Half of a Yellow Sun *by Chimananda Ngozi Adichie, Nigeria, 2006*

ICT – Information and communication technology

Importance

Information and communication technology is important for teaching and learning about equalities, difference and cohesion because it enables children to:

■ make confident, creative and productive use of ICT as an essential skill for everyday life; for study, learning and leisure; for employment; and for participation and engagement in society

■ find, develop, analyse and present information

■ gain rapid access to ideas and experiences from a wide range of people, communities and cultures

■ collaborate and exchange information on a wide scale

■ understand social, ethical, legal and economic implications.

Reflections – 62

More and more powerful

Computer chips are getting smaller and smaller and more and more powerful all the time. They're improving faster than any other machine in history. It's been calculated that if cars had developed at the same rate as computers over the last thirty years you'd be able to buy a Rolls Royce today for under a pound, and it would do three million miles to the gallon.

– from Thinks *by David Lodge*

Key concepts

Key concepts in ICT include:

Capability – using a range of ICT tools in a purposeful way to tackle questions, solve problems and create ideas and solutions of value.

Communication and collaboration – exploring the ways that ICT can be used to communicate and collaborate and share ideas on a global scale.

Critical evaluation – recognising that information must not be taken at face value but must be analysed and evaluated to take account of its purpose, provenance, currency and context, and reviewing and reflecting critically on what they and others produce using ICT.

Reflections – 63

Negative propaganda

– Before the net, it was much easier to know who to trust. Newspapers, books and TV news didn't always get their facts right, but you had a good idea who was writing the news and whether it was true or false. On the web it's more difficult. Because anyone can register a domain name, there are many examples of companies registering well-known names or brands to buy your trust. For example, if you visit the website www.martinlutherking.org, you might expect officially authorised information about Dr King. It's actually put up by Stormfront, a white supremacist organisation, to spread negative propaganda.

– advice at www.parentcentre.gov.uk

Key processes

Key processes and skills in ICT include:

■ analysing systematically the information requirements to solve a range of problems

■ selecting appropriate information from a wide range of sources, and judging the value, accuracy, plausibility and bias of information

■ selecting and using, with increasing integration and efficiency, the appropriate ICT tools for given problems

■ using ICT safely, securely and responsibly

■ evaluating one's experiences of using ICT, and considering the range of its uses and its significance to individuals, communities and society.

Classroom activities

Evaluation of websites

Pupils evaluate a range of websites about equality and diversity issues, considering features of style, navigation and content. They use this information to plan and design their own website about justice and diversity for a particular audience. They produce a project plan, breaking down work into a series of smaller tasks. In their work they consider efficiency, fitness for purpose and audience needs. For example, they might use ICT to convert and compress graphic files to allow faster download times. They make informed use of automated features in software to create a navigational menu on each page. Where appropriate, they integrate applications. For example, they may include a response form on their site, to collect information from users. They test and refine their site using the school intranet.

Visits to museums and exhibitions

Pupils plan a real or imaginary day trip to a museum specialising in issues of cultural diversity and equality, for example the Museum of the British Empire and Commonwealth at Bristol. They use the internet and paper-based materials to find out the entry fees and use route-finding software to determine the distance. They then enter this data into a spreadsheet model prepared in collaboration with the teacher and add data on cost of transport. They use the model to establish the cost per person. The teacher then provides a number of possible scenarios, for example an increase in the number of people, and pupils explore the model to provide answers. Groups make presentations to the rest of the class about their preferred destinations.

Reflections – 64

Signed stories

A new website aims to help improve the literacy of deaf children by allowing them to share in the joy of storytelling.

The Signed Stories site has been created to address the widening attainment gap at GCSE between deaf and hearing children and is a collaboration led by ITV, with the National Deaf Children's Society, eight UK publishers, teachers of the deaf, the National Literacy Trust and others. Each story is signed and also has the text read aloud, so it can be enjoyed by hearing and deaf readers alike.

The stories include well-known titles such as 'Not now, Bernard' and are presented in child-friendly categories including 'slimy scary'. There is also information for parents/carers and teachers on how to help deaf and hearing-impaired children (and parents) to be involved in story-telling.

– news item, March 2009

Campaigning for justice

Working in pairs, pupils create a web page about a particularly important movement, campaign or personality in the development of greater equality and justice. They need to research the subject and then write a short introduction identifying key facts and concepts, for example, Who? What? When? Where? Why? They also find or create between one and three images that can be scanned in to illustrate their text.

Living in Britain today

Pupils create powerpoint presentations or blogs about themselves using a range of software applications. They consider what helps to create their individual identities, and express their thoughts and feelings about living in Britain today. The subject-matter includes life events, family, friends and relationships, journeys, faith and religion, culture and celebrations, ethnicity, living with disability, sexual orientation, special skills and interests, the local neighbourhood, family history, and a sense of place and belonging.

Stories and books

Pupils visit the YouTube channel or the *Equally Different* area of the Equality and Human Rights Commission and view the video-portraits of a range of individuals in modern Britain. They create similar stories about real or imagined people, planning and drafting their texts with word-processing software. This enables them to work more efficiently and accurately than on paper since they can easily revert to previously saved versions. Once their texts are finished they use desktop-publishing software to create final books and include pictures and illustrations taken from a free online picture library. Their books are displayed at a local public library.

Combating cyberbullying

Pupils create web-based guidance on the nature and effects of cyberbullying, particularly cyberbullying which is prejudice-related (see pages 29-34 of this book). The material is perhaps divided into three broad sections: understanding, responding and preventing. It contains stories about the devastating effects of cyberbullying and provides advice on how pupils can support each other in challenging those who perpetrate it, and in building resilience and defiance amongst those who are at the receiving end.

Mathematics

Importance

Mathematics is important for teaching and learning about equalities, difference and cohesion because it enables children to:

- appreciate that mathematics is an international language, since it transcends cultural boundaries and its importance is universally recognised

- take part in public decision-making and the knowledge economy

- learn how to structure and organise their thoughts, handle information and make sense of data

- think independently in applied and abstract ways, and reason, solve problems and assess risks

- think logically, creatively and critically

- discern patterns, sort, classify, order, predict outcomes and learn the importance of accuracy.

Reflections – 65

Supreme beauty

Mathematics, rightly viewed, possesses not only truth but supreme beauty – a beauty cold and austere, like that of sculpture.

– *Bertrand Russell (1872-1970)*

Key concepts

Key concepts in mathematics include:

Competence – applying suitable mathematics accurately within the classroom and beyond, and selecting appropriate mathematical tools and methods, including ICT.

Creativity – combining understanding, experiences, imagination and reasoning to construct new knowledge.

Applications and implications of mathematics – knowing that mathematics is a rigorous, coherent discipline; understanding mathematics is used as a tool in a wide range of contexts; and recognising the rich historical and cultural roots of mathematics.

Reflections – 66

The tension between east and west

One of the great collaborations in the history of mathematics was between Geoffrey Harold Hardy, a professor at Cambridge, and Srinivasa Ramanujan, who worked as a clerk in Madras, India. They corresponded with each other and Ramanujan joined Hardy in Cambridge for a while in the period 1915-1920.

It was a real culture clash, like trying to marry the traditions of western classical music with the ragas and talas of India. This tension between east and west is one which runs throughout much of mathematical history. For many like Hardy, mathematics was regarded as a European endeavour dating back to the traditions of Ancient Greece. The influence of other cultures has received little recognition. But many of the great mathematical ideas, such as the concept of zero and the potency of infinite sums, have their origins in India.

Ramanujan returned to India after the end of the First World War... The last letter he wrote to Hardy in 1920 was full of talk of a new mathematical idea he called a mock theta function and it was away ahead of its time. Only in the past few years has a full understanding of Ramanujan's function become clear: Kathrin Bringmann and Ken Ono of the University of Wisconsin have given the first complete explanation of the ideas contained in that last letter. It is striking in a world dominated by men that a woman has been a key character in illuminating Ramanujan's work.

– from the introduction by Marcus du Sautoy to A Disappearing Number *devised by the Complicité theatre company. 2007*

Critical understanding – knowing that mathematics is essentially abstract and can be used to model, interpret or represent situations, and recognising the limitations and scope of a model or representation.

Key processes

Key processes and skills in mathematics include:

- identifying the mathematical aspects of a situation or problem and simplifying the situation or problem in order to represent it mathematically, using appropriate variables, symbols, diagrams and models

- visualising and working with dynamic images, identifying and classifying patterns, and making and justifying conjectures and generalisations, whilst bearing in mind special cases and counter-examples

- exploring the effects of varying values and looking for invariance and covariance

- making accurate mathematical diagrams, graphs and constructions on paper and on screen

- calculating accurately, selecting mental methods or calculating devices as appropriate

- manipulating numbers, algebraic expressions and equations, and applying routine algorithms

- being aware of the strength of empirical evidence and appreciate the difference between evidence and proof

- engaging with someone else's mathematical reasoning in the context of a problem or particular situation

Classroom activities

Global village

Pupils work with the picture book *If the World were a Village* by David Smith and present the same statistical data in alternative forms. The topics include nationalities, languages, ages, religions, air and water, schooling and literacy, money and possessions, electricity, food, and past and present. There are many classroom activities suggested at acblack.com/globalvillage.

Identities, belongings and statistics

Pupils work with data and materials at the Census at School website, based at Nottingham Trent University (www.censusatschool.ntu.ac.uk). There are questionnaires for them to fill in, downloadable worksheets, an interactive histogram, a poem, a song, factsheets about the 2001 census of population, and a wealth of activities integrating statistical analysis with geography, history, science, ICT and citizenship. There are sister sites in Canada, New Zealand, Queensland and South Australia.

Demography

Pupils use from data published by the Office of National Statistics relating to the 2001 census of population and construct, on paper and using ICT, a range of graphs and charts and identify which styles of numerical representation are most suitable for various purposes and contexts. They then present concise, reasoned arguments, using symbols, diagrams, graphs and related explanatory text. They engage in similar tasks using data from the Women and Work Commission and factsheets issued by the former Equal Opportunities Commission.

The state of the nation

Working in groups, pupils assemble mathematical illustrations of propositions in official reports and design tests which would establish whether the situation is improving or getting worse. For example, they consider statements in DCSF documents on education or in *The State of the Nation* by the Institute for Public Policy Research. The latter is downloadable from www.ippr.org.uk. It contains statistics on wealth and income distribution, social mobility, crime and fear of crime, differentials in the pay of women and men, and levels of child poverty in UK and other European countries.

Modern foreign languages

Importance

Modern foreign languages are important for teaching and learning about equalities, difference and cohesion because they enable children to:

- appreciate different countries, cultures, communities and people

- gain insight into their own culture and society

- become more aware of their own identity and culture, as well as developing greater empathy and respect for other people

- develop a lifelong skill for education, employment and leisure both in their own country and throughout the world

- develop awareness of the changing nature of language, of borrowings between different languages, and of the relationship between language and reality.

- learn how language can be manipulated and applied in different ways.

Key concepts

Key concepts in modern foreign languages include:

Linguistic competence – developing the skills of listening, speaking, reading and writing in a range of situations and contexts

> *Reflections – 67*
> ### Rarely a suggestion
> Many courses use scenarios that invite learners to imagine visiting a country associated with the target language and attempt to give the learner a role as actor in an intercultural setting. However, since the purpose imagined for the visit is often tourism, the language learner is often represented in course material not as a citizen but as a child within the family, pupil within the school and consumer within society. There is rarely a suggestion that students will take with them any curiosity or any social, historical, economic or political awareness.
>
> *– Hugh Starkey, 2005*

> *Reflections – 68*
> ### Past, present, future
> Teaching past, present and future tenses becomes more meaningful when students study the past, present and future of global issues. This can involve students in studying the historical background of an issue such as environmental pollution in their community or country, then doing future-oriented activities concerned with solving this problem. Comparatives can similarly be practised through comparing human rights in different countries, and global inequalities of First World wealth and Third World poverty. Some teachers have designed exercises to teach students the conditional 'if — then' while promoting environmental awareness. These revolve around pattern practice based on model sentences such as 'If we recycled paper we'd save more trees; or 'If we all picked up litter at our university, we'd have a beautiful clean campus,'
>
> *– Kip Cates, 2005*

Knowledge about language – understanding how a language works and how to manipulate it, and recognising that languages differ but may share common grammatical, syntactical or lexical features

Creativity – using familiar language for new purposes and in new contexts, and using imagination to express thoughts, ideas, experiences and feelings

Intercultural understanding – Recognising that there are different ways of seeing the world, appreciating the distinctive features of one's own culture as also those of others.

Key processes

Key processes and skills in the study of modern languages include:

- identifying patterns in the target language

- developing techniques for memorising words, phrases and spellings

- using one's knowledge of English or another language when learning the target language

- using previous knowledge, context and other clues to work out the meaning of what one hears or reads.

Classroom activities

Interpreting course

Pupils with oral fluency in a language other than English are given training to develop their skills so that they can act as interpreters at parents evenings. This involves agreement on whether and how to translate specialist terms and ethical issues around impartiality and confidentiality. The course forms part of the school's curriculum enrichment programme and is linked with a university-run scheme. It leads to a certificate recognised by UCAS and can therefore help students to gain a university place.

Sign language

Pupils are introduced to British Sign Language. They learn basic conversational phrases, and appreciate BSL's grammatical features and structures. They practise with DVDs and various specialist websites, and meet and converse with deaf people and BSL translators. They may compare and contrast BSL with American Sign Language.

Induction course

An induction course in modern foreign languages is taught before focusing on one language in particular. There is an emphasis on transferable language-learning skills and on awareness of the ways in which languages work. Pupils explore the relationships between different languages, including links between Asian and European languages, and the cultural and social contexts in which language is used.

Timeline

Pupils create a timeline showing the arrival of various new words in English from other languages over the centuries, including words originally coined in America and other English-speaking countries and now part of world English.

On va visiter la Côte d'Ivoire

Pupils go on an imaginary trip to a Francophone country: *Nous allons visiter la Suisse/La Martiniqu/ le Canada/ la Côte d'Ivoire. C'est une bonne idée? Qui a un passeport?* Real timetables are used to revise telling the time, and there is talk about how long it takes to get to a place. Each pupil makes their own 'passport', with relevant details, and writes a personal biography based on the book *L'Histoire de Ma Vie* by Ulfet Mahmout and Alan Thompson, published by Mantra Books. In an imaginary airport waiting room the flight is announced (*Air France annonce le vol 345 à destination Montréal. Les passagers sont priés de se rendre à la porte numéro 6*) and once inside the 'aircraft' the teacher takes the role of flight attendant and acts out simplified safety precautions. Scrapbooks and diaries are compiled about the trip, in English as well as in French.

Seven world languages

Pupils collect basic information (history, number of speakers, places spoken, unique features, distinctive vowel and consonant sounds, writing system, well-known proverbs, basic courtesies and greetings, puns, political slogans, borrowings from other languages) in seven world languages: Arabic, Chinese, German, French, Russian, Spanish and Urdu/Hindi. They listen to tape-recorded examples of these languages and learn to recognise them. Also, they learn to recognise the written forms of the languages, and practise writing them themselves.

Reflections – 69

Comprendo

Lev shook his head, trying to show her she'd read him wrong, that he was a good man, a loving father, but this shaking of his head alarmed the woman and she called to her friends: 'He's not going. Someone call the police.'

'No,' said Lev. 'No police.'

'Then leave.'

'I am new,' said Lev. 'I am only looking my way through many streets.'

The woman sighed, as one of her friends joined her. 'Nutter,' she said. 'Foreign nutter. Probably harmless.'

'OK,' said the friend, approaching Lev. 'Pissez-off Right? Comprendo?'

from The Road Home *by Rose Tremain, 2007*

Music

Importance

Music is important for teaching and learning about equalities, difference and cohesion because it enables children to:

- gain a lively sense of aspirations, needs, problems and desires that all human beings have in common

- learn to appreciate and value the specific and distinctive nature of musical genres across times and cultures, and to understand the contexts in which they were made

- develop confidence, competence, imagination, self-management and creativity in exploring and expressing their own identities

- reflect critically on their own and other people's work, judging quality, value and meaning

- take risks and learn from their mistakes

- appreciate the role that music plays in the creative and cultural industries that enrich and shape their lives, and influence the views they have of themselves and others.

Key concepts

Key concepts in the study of music include:

Participation – collaborating and working with others as musicians, adapting to different musical roles and respecting the values and benefits others bring to musical learning.

Cultural understanding – the part music plays in national and global culture and in personal identity; exploring how ideas, experiences and emotions are conveyed in a range of music from different times and cultures.

Critical understanding – drawing on experience of a wide range of musical contexts and styles to inform judgments.

Creativity – using existing musical knowledge, skills and understanding for new purposes and in new contexts, and exploring ways music can be combined with other art forms and other subject disciplines.

Communication – appreciating how thoughts, feelings, ideas and emotions can be expressed through music.

Reflections – 70

I want to be part

Into my mind comes an extraordinarily beautiful sound. I am nine years old. I am sitting between Mr and Mrs Formby in a state of anticipation. On the seats all around us are people chattering and rustling programmes. Into the circus ring enter not elephants and lions but a group of men and women, many of them bearing amazing instruments, gleaming and glowing. A small, frail man enters to applause such as I have never heard before, followed by the strange, absolute silence of a multitude.

He brings down a stick and a huge and lovely noise fills the world. More than anything else I want to be part of such a noise.

– *from* Silent Music *by Vikram Seth*

Reflections – 71

Do what you can

People talk to me about success as if I know what it is, but I think success is what you feel when you are in your late 50s, with your feet up and a glass of whiskey in your hand. I'm not sure of the process. I'm still at the beginning of what I'm doing ... Right now, I feel on my own and I don't feel anybody is really lumped together. I think that, maybe at the beginning, people thought I was one thing ... and I wasn't. It's quite exciting to keep people surprised and I look forward to doing that. ... It's more exciting to look back at stuff from 40 or 50 years ago, than 20 years ago. Every time I'm in America, I feel there's some atmosphere – I can't put my finger on it – but there's some excitement that exists nowhere else. And I think it's because soul music, black music, is basically what started pop music ...The most important thing in music is honesty, because that basically accomplishes everything. You might not be the best singer, or show your emotions the way you wish you could, but if you're honest, you ultimately do what you can.

– *from an interview with Duffy, autumn 2008*

Key processes

Key processes and skills in music include:

- singing in solo or group contexts, developing vocal techniques and musical expression

- perform with control of instrument-specific techniques and musical expression

- creating, developing and extending musical ideas by selecting and combining resources within musical structures, styles, genres and traditions

- improvising, exploring and developing musical ideas when performing

- identifying conventions and contextual influences in music of different styles, genres and traditions

- communicating ideas and feelings about music, using expressive language and musical vocabulary to justify one's opinions

- adapting one's own musical ideas and refining and improving one's own and others' work.

Reflections – 72

Many dialects

The generation that has grown up with the sounds of the music of the last fifty years outside the classical tradition has been exposed to a richer and broader range of music than any other in history. It has absorbed inventive rock, maybe some experimental electronic music, heard sounds from traditions from around the world that weren't available in earlier times, learned that musical language has many dialects. That will leave its mark ... The history of music-making is evidence that the ebb and flow of taste in the audience and invention among composers is the way of the world ... the urge to create music of originality and power will not be stifled ... music-makers will write and perform because it is as natural to them as to breathe, and their power will survive.

– closing sentences of The Making of Music by James Naughtie, 2007

Classroom activities

Story in sound

Pupils tell a story in sound about an encounter between two or more cultures, or else in response to an event of local, national or international importance. They explain the original musical ideas, how they were developed and why some of the musical features were chosen. If songs are used, either familiar or specially composed, there is consideration, discussion and appraisal of pitch, duration, dynamics, diction and phrasing.

Choral music

Pupils perform the gospel melody *Standing in the need of prayer* and add harmony parts that a) move in parallel and b) are modified to fit with conventional harmonies. They listen to gospel music from South Africa, London and the United States, focusing on ways in which changes of texture create variety and interest, and listen with a similar focus to traditional choral pieces from New Zealand, Bulgaria and Pakistan. Finally, they arrange a group performance of a gospel melody and compose their own a-cappela pieces incorporating idiomatic features of one of the styles which they have studied.

Muslim hip hop and points arising

Young people listen to various Muslim rappers and visit their websites, and look at some of the debates that have taken place, and continue to take place within Muslim communities, about whether Islam and Hip Hop music are compatible. If their judgement is that there is no inherent incompatibility, they compose, perform and record their own work.

Reviewing

Pupils listen to, for example, *London Undersound* by Nitin Sawhney (2008) and compare their own reactions with those of a BBC reviewer (Chris Jones): '...For younger Londoners one gets the feeling that this cultural smorgasbord may be a little too smooth ... You won't find grime creeping in here. Musically, Sawhney is a polymath, but his brew sometimes seems too safe .... Such a huge city contains far more than his blend of flamenco, beats and Asian signifiers ... bejewelled and intricate but one longs for some grit ... Too polite to convey the anger, tension, sense of betrayal and essentially contradictory nature of living in the nation's capital in 2008 ... an album with its heart firmly in the right place, but lacking in bite.

Physical education

Importance

Physical education is important for teaching and learning about equalities, difference and cohesion because it enables children to:

- develop competence and confidence to take part in a range of physical activities that become a central part of their lives, both in and out of school

- develop a wide range of skills and the ability to use tactics, strategies and compositional ideas to perform successfully

- learn about the value of healthy, active lifestyles, discovering what they like to do, what their aptitudes are at school, and how and where to get involved in physical activity

- make informed choices about lifelong physical activity

- work as individuals, in groups and teams, developing concepts of fairness and personal and social responsibility

- take on different roles and responsibilities, including leadership, coaching and officiating.

Reflections – 73

All I know

All I know most surely about morality and obligations, I owe to football.

– *Albert Camus, Nobel prize for literature, 1957*

I tend to think that cricket is the greatest thing that God created on earth.

– *Harold Pinter, Nobel prize for literature, 2005*

Key concepts

Key concepts in physical education include:

Competence – developing control of whole-body skills and fine manipulation skills, and selecting and using skills, tactics and compositional ideas effectively in different types of physical activity; responding with body and mind to the demands of an activity; adapting to a widening range of familiar and unfamiliar contexts.

Performance – understanding how the components of competence combine, and applying them to produce effective outcomes; knowing and understanding what needs to be achieved, critically evaluating how well it has been achieved and finding ways to improve; appreciating how to make adjustments and adaptations when performing in different contexts and when working individually, in groups and teams.

Creativity – using imaginative ways to express and communicate ideas, solve problems and overcome challenges; exploring and experimenting with techniques, tactics and compositional ideas to produce efficient and effective outcomes.

Healthy, active lifestyles – understanding that physical activity contributes to the healthy functioning of the body and mind and is an essential component of a healthy lifestyle; recognising that regular physical activity that is fit for purpose, safe and enjoyable has the greatest impact on physical, mental and social wellbeing.

Key processes

Key processes and skills in physical education include:

- refining and adapting skills into techniques

- developing the precision, control and fluency of their skills

- selecting and using tactics, strategies and compositional ideas effectively in different creative, competitive and challenging contexts

- planning and implementing what needs practising to be more effective in performance

- recognising hazards and making decisions about how to control risks to oneself and others

- developing physical strength, stamina, speed and flexibility to cope with the demands of different activities

- analysing performances, identifying strengths and weaknesses with a view to making improvements

- identifying the types of activity they are best suited to, and the types of role they would like to take on

- making choices about their involvement in healthy physical activity.

Reflections – 74

Teenage years

Girls will continue to play sport into their teens if they can wear fashionable black and pink hoodies and tracksuit bottoms instead of pleated skirts, shorts or white T-shirts, says Dame Kelly Holmes, who today launches a prototype for the ideal modern PE kit.

After speaking to girls across the country, the Olympic gold medallist argues that more traditional uniform puts girls off because it is 'uncool'. They are also embarrassed about revealing their legs and fear white T-shirts are see-through. A shift away from the shorts, traditional hockey skirts, white socks and baggy polo shirts could revolutionise girls' sport, Holmes concluded.

What girls wear 'is the main area that needs to be tackled and may help lower teenage dropout rates from physical activities', she said. 'Modern teenagers need to feel comfortable, so they are less conscious of their body image. Primarily they want tracksuits for outside activities and to cover their legs, hoodies for team sports and colour-coded T-shirts. The colours that have come out on top have been black with pink writing or logos.'

Holmes has visited a number of schools where girls' plans to transform PE have particularly impressed her. The visits are part of the Norwich Union GirlsActive programme, a government initiative sponsored by the insurance company which aims to reverse a trend that has seen 40 per cent of girls drop out of all sports in their teenage years. Holmes had highlighted clothing, changing rooms and type of sports as areas she wanted to investigate, but has now concluded that PE kit is the key.

– news item, January 2008

Classroom activities

Wall of stars

Pupils prepare a wall of sporting heroes. A large wallspace is selected and covered with sugar paper and over the period of a sporting season, pupils build up a collage of pictures and words. They bring in photographs of their heroes and heroines, and paste them onto the wall. They also paste up quotations, perhaps using the antiracist football websites to help them. Also they write their own words or poems to add to the wall. The display features both women and men; athletes who are disabled; athletes who are or are said to be gay; and athletes from a range of ethnic and religious backgrounds.

Code of practice

Pupils visit websites such as Kick It Out, Show Racism the Red Card, and Football Unites Racism Divides, run by Sheffield United. They make a list of issues relating to the eradication of racism on football terraces and in football management. They draw up a code of conduct for their own school, including in this the school playground as well as official games, and include in this issues of disability equality, homophobia and sexism.

Kiddiesville

Pupils visit the website of Kiddiesville Football Club, and note its themes relating to disability, ethnicity and gender. They write additional poems and songs, and press reports on matches against opponents.

Paralympics

In the run-up to 2012, pupils take a special interest in the Paralympics, using a wide range of resources, research projects, websites and blogs.

Biographies

Pupils research the lives and achievements of specific individuals, for example Amir Khan, using material on The Red Card website, also in Red Card's Islamophobia pack, or Ade Adepitan, using a film about him made by Teachers TV.

Skill and strategy

Pupils play broadly similar games from two or more different cultures and note the similarities and variations in terms of skill, purpose and strategy. Instead or as well, girls play games that are traditionally played only or mainly by boys, and boys play games that are traditionally played only or mainly by girls.

PSHEE – Personal, social, health and economic education

Importance

Personal, social, health and economic education is important for teaching and learning about equalities, difference and cohesion because it enables children to:

- embrace change, feel positive about who they are and enjoy healthy, safe and responsible lives

- recognise and manage risk, take increasing responsibility for themselves, their choices and behaviours

- make positive contributions to their families, schools and communities

- appreciate they belong to a range of groups and are formed by a range of influences, and have to balance loyalties that sometimes conflict

- consider social and moral dilemmas in everyday life and in local, national and global politics

- manage new or difficult situations positively and form and maintain effective relationships

Key concepts

Career – developing a sense of personal identity for career progression, and understanding how to make creative and realistic plans for transition.

Risk – understanding risk in both positive and negative terms, and the need to manage risk in the context of personal relationships and group memberships and in financial and career choices; learning from one's mistakes.

Economic understanding – understanding the economic and business environment and the functions and uses of money.

Diversity – appreciating similarities and differences amongst people in relation to age, disability, ethnicity, faith, gender and sexuality.

Reflections – 75

Mixture

I am a Glaswegian Pakistani teenage woman of Muslim descent, who supports Glasgow Rangers in a Catholic school, 'cause I'm a mixture and I'm proud of it.

Reflections – 76

The heart of every human being

If only there were evil people somewhere insidiously committing evil deeds, and it were necessary only to separate them from the rest of us and destroy them. But the line dividing good and evil cuts through the heart of every human being: and who is willing to destroy a piece of his own heart?

– The Gulag Archipelago *by Alexander Solzenitsyn*

Equality – understanding all forms of prejudice and discrimination must be challenged at every level of one's life.

Key processes

Key processes and skills in PSHEE include:

- developing and maintaining one's self-esteem and envisaging a positive future

- assessing one's needs, interests, values, skills, abilities and attitudes in relation to options in learning, work and enterprise

- dealing with growth and change as normal parts of growing up.

- understanding that relationship skills have to be learnt and practised.

Reflections – 77

The big picture of their lives

The Challenging Violence, Changing Lives programme was primarily delivered in PSHEE lessons – the subject that addresses rites of passage into adulthood, sexual and social identities and healthy relationships. Our evaluation clearly establishes that young people do not view these issues as separate to their education, but integral to it, and view them within the big picture of their lives. The programme had most impact in schools when gender equality issues and PSHEE content were already being integrated into the broader fabric of the school.

– Womankind UK, 2007

Classroom activities
What next?

Pupils discuss real or imagined incidents where there is uncertainty about what should happen next. They write letters or messages to a helpline, blog or agony column, and discuss and draft possible answers. Also, they consider where they themselves would turn for advice, assistance and guidance on matters such those raised by the stories. They evaluate the real answers given on similar topics in magazines and on websites.

Living and learning

Pupils are given about six short extracts from biographical writings, and draw up lists of questions they would like to ask if they had the opportunity to meet the people who are featured in the writings. They then convert these into real interview schedules and use the schedules to interview certain individuals. They may then write similar pieces themselves, or create video diaries, or create profiles of themselves on Facebook or Bebo.

Sibel's story

Pupils use a Persona doll to construct and tell the story of Sibel, a five year old from Iran whose family is seeking asylum in the UK. Information is provided by the teacher about reasons for leaving Iran and the dangerous journey to the UK. Imaginary family photographs are found on the internet and culturally relevant artefacts such as clothing are obtained from friends. Commonalities between Sibel and the pupils are established, for example with regard to the likes, dislikes and worries of any five year old girl in the world. Cultural, linguistic and religious diversity are considered. (For further information and ideas, visit the website of Portsmouth Ethnic Minority Support Service at www.blss.portsmouth.sch.uk/ default.htm.)

Moral courage

Pupils investigate the story of Rosa Parks and her role in the early days of the civil rights movement in the United States. (Useful books at key stages 1 and 2 include *The Bus Ride* by William Miller and *A Picture Book of Rosa Parks* by David Adler.) They discuss the concept of moral courage, using materials developed by the Anne Frank Trust UK and available at www.annefrank.org.uk, and make real or imagined entries for the Anne Frank Moral Courage Awards programme. They sign up to the Anne Frank Declaration and create posters about this for the classroom and school corridors.

Gender roles in childhood

Pupils work with a selection of birthday cards addressed to family members – 'To my daughter' , 'To my dad', and so on, and cards welcoming a new baby. What are the assumptions and expectations that are expressed about gender roles and qualities? They work also with advertisements for toys. Are certain toys clearly marketed for one gender or the other? They construct and administer a questionnaire to investigate whether they and their peers hold the same assumptions as those that are made in the cards and advertisements. Finally, they write letters to card and toy manufacturers with their observations, and collate the replies they receive.

Identities

In groups, pupils research concepts of identity, belonging and community, using a range of sources of information, including the Britkids website. Each group feeds back to the rest of the class and discuss what they have found out and discuss diversity in Britain in the twenty-first century. Finally, each imagines identity as a mask that reflects aspects of heritage or community, and designs and creates a mask to reflect their loyalties and affiliations.

The character Croc

Croc (the key character in Lift Off, devised for human rights education in primary schools) is from another planet and comes to Planet Earth to find out how humans live. Croc's questions include: What do humans need to live long, healthy and happy lives? What responsibilities go hand in hand with having rights? What do humans do when there is a conflict of rights? (full information at the Lift Off website, address on page 85.

Religious education

Importance

Religious education is important for teaching and learning about equalities, difference and cohesion because it enables children to:

- gain a lively sense of aspirations, needs, problems and desires that all human beings have in common

- develop their awareness and understanding of religions and beliefs, teachings, practices and forms of expression

- explore the differences between superstition and religion

- learn from different religions, beliefs, values and traditions, while exploring their own beliefs and questions of meaning. It challenges pupils to reflect on, consider, analyse, interpret and evaluate issues of truth, belief, faith and ethics and to communicate their responses

- study ways in which religious ideas and structures have sometimes been used in the past, and are still used in the present, to justify prejudices and discrimination, for example in relation to disabilities, gender and ethnicity.

Key concepts

Key concepts in religious education include:

Beliefs, teachings and sources – including systems of thought that are religious and non-religious, theistic and non-theistic, Western and Eastern, Abrahamic and dharmic.

Change, diversity and interaction – understanding that religious practices are diverse, change over time and are influenced by cultures.

Impact – exploring the impact of religions and beliefs on how people live their lives, understanding how moral values and a sense of obligation can come from beliefs and experience.

Identity, diversity and belonging – understanding how individuals develop a sense of identity and belonging through faith or belief.

Meaning, purpose and truth – exploring some of the ultimate questions that confront humanity, and responding imaginatively to them.

Key processes

Key skills and processes in religious education include:

- appreciating and practising the range of ways that religious beliefs are expressed, including writing, speech, silence, symbol, metaphor, art, music, myth, story, song, dress, dance, food, ritual, artefacts, relationships, behaviour codes and social action

---

Reflections – 78

No superiority

Allah says, 'O People, We have created you from one male and one female and made you into tribes and nations, that you may know one another. Verily, in the sight of Allah, the most honoured amongst you is the one who is most God-fearing. There is no superiority for an Arab over a non-Arab or for non-Arab over an Arab, nor for the white over the black, nor for the black over the white, except in God-consciousness.

Final Sermon of the Prophet Muhammad, c. 630 CE

Reflections – 79

Always sides with the little ones

God was entirely on Alice's side. God always sides with the little ones, children over adults, the sick over the healthy, the minorities over the powerful. Felicity did not see this in terms of politics, in terms of Liberation theology ... but in terms of relationships. God loved her and God loved Alice, but in any struggle He would side with Alice, because Alice was deaf. It was this knowledge, this certainty that made it possible for her to fight so hard for Alice, but the same certainty made it impossible for her to fight for herself ... Over the last months she had had to dodge God. She had even tried persuading herself that God did not exist; but she could not convince herself. God existed all right and wanted more from Felicity than she had to give. 'It's not fair,' she wanted to scream ... she was too lazy, too greedy, too selfish, to have a child that was not of her choosing.

from Home Truths *by Sara Maitland, 1993*

- engaging in dialogue, and understanding the differences between dialogue and conversation, and dialogue and persuasion

- applying a wide range of religious and philosophical vocabulary consistently and accurately, recognising both the power and the limitations of language in expressing religious ideas and beliefs

Classroom activities

Reviewing a project

Pupils visit the website of the Tanenbaum Center and make a note of projects that catch their interest. They then choose one of these to focus on, listing what they see as the strengths and advantages of the project, noting any reservations or criticisms they may have, and listing the questions they would like to ask if there were a chance of speaking and meeting with a representative of the project. They then make links with similar questions to projects in the school's local neighbourhood.

To be a British Muslim

Pupils attend to the testimony and experience of young British Muslims, as outlined and discussed on the websites of *Muslim News, Q News* and the Muslim Council of Britain, and in the 2004 report of the Commission on British Muslims and Islamophobia. They identify commonalities, similarities and differences in the lives and identities of British Christians, British Jews and British Sikhs, and also look at dual identities such as Black British, Scottish British, Mancunian British.

Problem or solution?

Pupils debate three 'Big Myths' set out in *Connect: different faiths, shared values*, published by the Inter Faith Network in association with TimeBank and the National Youth Agency in 2004. The myths are (1) 'Well, they may say they're religious but no-one believes any of that stuff' (2) 'Religious people are just a bunch of fanatics' and (3) 'Religion divides people – all the religions hate each other'. They then sort through some of the stories and case studies in the *Connect* booklet about practical inter-faith projects in various parts of Britain. For each project they ask and consider three questions: What do you see as the strengths of this project? What reservations or criticisms do you have? If you could meet someone from the project what would you ask?

Fool, trickster, rogue or sage?

Pupils read or enact a number of Mullah Nasruddin stories, and re-tell some of them using modern contexts and references. Which stories show a foolish or ignorant person, which show a trickster, which a rogue, a wise person? Do some show all four? Can they summarise the teachings in the stories with pithy sayings of their own devising? Instead or as well, which pithy or proverbial sayings, in a collection provided for them, do they consider most relevant to summarise each story?

Reflections – 80

Also our mother

Just as God is our Father, so God is also our Mother. And He showed me this truth in all things, but especially in those sweet words when He says: 'It is I'. As if to say, 'I am the power and the Goodness of the Father, I am the Wisdom of the Mother, I am the Light and the Grace which is blessed love, I am the Trinity, I am the Unity, I am the supreme Goodness of all kind of things, I am the One who makes you love, I am the One who makes you desire, I am the never-ending fulfilment of all true desires.

Julian of Norwich, 14th century

Reflections – 81

Both critical and respectful

Religious education can make it less likely that religious young people and adults will become fanatical, and that the residual spirituality of secularised people will be more resistant to political and social parties who seek to stir up traditional folk religiosity ... We want to help people (including ourselves) to be thoughtful and socially responsible in their religious living, if they are religious, and not to be prejudiced or patronising toward religion if they are not religious themselves. Religious education is not a religion but it seeks to promote an understanding of religion which is both critical and respectful.

John Hull, 2006

Science

Importance

Science is important for teaching and learning about equalities, difference and cohesion because it enables children to

- appreciate how knowledge and understanding in science are rooted in evidence, and that science is a universal human activity

- see how scientific ideas contribute to technological change, affecting industry, business and medicine and improving quality of life

- use experimentation and modelling to develop and evaluate explanations, encouraging critical and creative thought

- trace the development of science worldwide and recognise its cultural significance

- question and discuss issues that may affect their own lives, the directions of societies and the future of the world.

Key concepts

Key concepts in science include:

Scientific thinking – using scientific ideas and models to explain phenomena and developing them creatively to generate and test hypotheses, and critically analysing and evaluating evidence from observations and experiments.

Applications and implications of science – exploring how the creative application of scientific ideas can bring about technological developments and consequent changes in the way people think and behave, and examining the ethical and moral implications of using and applying science.

Cultural understanding – recognising that modern science has its roots in a wide range of societies and cultures, and draws on a varied range of valid approaches to scientific practice.

Collaboration – sharing across disciplines and boundaries.

Reflections – 82

It must be done for itself

We must not forget that when radium was discovered no one knew that it would prove useful in hospitals. The work was one of pure science. And this is a proof that scientific work must not be considered from the point of view of the direct usefulness of it. It must be done for itself, for the beauty of science, and then there is always the chance that a scientific discovery may become like the radium a benefit for humanity.

– Marie Curie, 1921

Key processes

Key processes and skills in science include:

- using a range of scientific methods and techniques to develop and test ideas and explanations

- assessing risk and working safely in the laboratory, field or workplace

- planning and carrying out practical and investigative activities, both individually and in groups

- obtaining, recording and analysing data from a wide range of primary and secondary sources, including ICT sources, and using one's findings to provide evidence for scientific explanations

- evaluating scientific evidence and working methods

- using appropriate methods, including ICT, to communicate scientific information and contributing to presentations and discussions about scientific issues.

Reflections – 83

A hundred centuries of trial and error

... We began studying physics together, and Sandro was surprised when I tried to explain to him some of the ideas that at the time I was confusedly cultivating. That the nobility of man, acquired in a hundred centuries of trial and error, lay in making himself the conqueror of matter, and that I had enrolled in chemistry because I wanted to remain faithful to this nobility. That conquering matter is to understand it, and understanding matter is necessary to understanding the universe and ourselves...

... Finally, and fundamentally, an honest and open boy, did he not smell the stench of Fascist truths which tainted the sky? Did he not perceive it as an ignominy that a thinking man should be asked to believe without thinking? Was he not filled with disgust at all the dogmas, all the unproved affirmations, all the imperatives?

He did feel it; so then, how could he not feel a new dignity and majesty in our study, how could he ignore the fact that the chemistry and physics on which we fed, besides nourishments vital in themselves, were the antidote to Fascism which he and I were seeking, because they were clear and distinct and verifiable at every step, and not a tissue of lies and emptiness, like the radio and newspapers?

– The Periodic Table *by Primo Levi, , 1975. This part of the book is set in Italy in the 1930s.*

Classroom activities

Commonalities and differences

In a topic on *Ourselves*, pupils make surveys of various physical characteristics, including skin colour, eye colour, gender and height, and of personal interests, for example favourite foods, celebrities, music and pets, and draw Venn diagrams to show commonalities and differences.

The spread of knowledge

Pupils play a version of the game Woolly Thinking in order to study the spread of knowledge in the year 1000. The game vividly illustrates and dramatises interactions between China, India, the Middle East and Europe and portrays science as a universal human activity. Full instructions are on the website of the Muslim Home School Network, based in the United States, at http://www.muslimhomeschool.com – click on Pride and then on educational material. Pupils then explore the wealth of material about Muslim science at www.muslimheritage.com and the implications of such material for any British classroom today at the website of the Islamic Society of Britain (www.isb.org.uk and follow the links to the Virtual Classroom.)

Women in science, engineering and technology

Pupils familiarise themselves with facts and theory relating to the under-representation of women in science-based careers and make recommendations for action at their own school.

The context of scientific invention

In a topic on electrical circuits, pupils study the development of the electric lamp. They develop knowledge of the heating and lighting effect of a current; that resistance to a current depends on the type and thickness of the conducting material; that air is needed for things to burn (oxygen is the active ingredient); that the vacuum pump to remove air was invented; different materials were tested as filaments (eg metals, carbon); and that various techniques for holding the filaments were investigated.

Within this context pupils study the contributions of the great African American inventor Lewis Latimer (1848-1928). Latimer devised a way of encasing the filament within a cardboard envelope which prevented the carbon from breaking and thereby provided a much longer life to the bulb, so making them less expensive and more efficient. This enabled electric lighting to be installed in homes and throughout streets. Pupils become aware of the nature of scientific enquiry; the creativity, rivalries and competition involved in scientific invention and discovery; the cultural, social, economic and industrial circumstances in which scientific progress takes place and by which it is influenced; the struggle for due recognition of black inventors; and the nature and effects of institutional racism.

We can change the future

No scientific basis

'Daddy, people talk about the white race, the black race, the yellow race. We hear that at school. The teacher told us the other day that Abdou's race is black. He's from Mali.'

'If your teacher really said that, she was wrong. I hate to tell you this, because I know you like her, but she's wrong ... Human races don't exist. There is a human species in which there are men and women, people of colour, tall people and short people, with different strengths and weaknesses ...

The word 'race' has no scientific basis ... We shouldn't use physical differences – skin colour, height, facial features – to divide humanity hierarchically. That is, to claim that some people are better than others.'

– from Racism Explained To My Daughter *by Tahar Ben Jelloun, 1999*

The heart of enlightened Europe

The Holocaust did not happen far away, in some distant time and in another kind of civilization. It happened in the heart of enlightened Europe in a country that prided itself on its art, its culture, its philosophy and ethics. However painful it is, we must learn what happened, that it may never happen again to anyone, whatever their colour, culture or creed. We cannot change the past, but by remembering the past, we can change the future.

– Jonathan Sacks, Auschwitz, 13 November 2008

PART FOUR
Planning, legislation and resources

This section of the book provides information that will be useful for
undertaking practical next steps.

The first chapter offers a model school policy which schools may use a starting point or
set of prompts when developing their own such statements. The second sets out questions which
governing bodies and leadership teams may find useful when conducting self-evaluation exercises and
drawing up action plans. The third cites the exact terminology in legislation currently (2009) in force.
The fourth sketches the historical and international background to the legislation. Finally, there are
descriptions of about 70 useful websites, and notes on the references and
quotations used in the book.

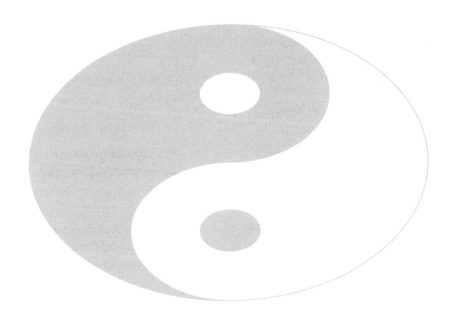

A model school policy

Legal duties

1. We welcome our duties under the Disability Discrimination Acts 1995 and 2005; the Race Relations Acts 1976 as amended by the Race Relations Amendment Act 2000; and the Sex Discrimination Act 1975 as amended by the Equality Act 2006.

2. We welcome our duty under the Education and Inspections Act 2006 to promote community cohesion.

3. We recognise that these four sets of duties are essential for achieving the five outcomes of the Every Child Matters framework, and that they reflect international human rights standards as expressed in the UN Convention on the Rights of the Child, the UN Convention on the Rights of People with Disabilities, and the Human Rights Act 1998.

4. Summaries of our legal obligations are provided in Appendix A.

Guiding principles

5. In fulfilling the legal obligations referred to above, and summarised in Appendix A, we are guided by seven principles:

    Principle 1: All pupils are of equal value
    We see all pupils and potential pupils, and their parents and carers, as of equal value:

    ☐ whether or not they are disabled

    ☐ whatever their ethnicity, culture, religious affiliation, national origin or national status

    ☐ whichever their gender.

    Principle 2: We recognise and respect difference
    Treating people equally does not necessarily involve treating them all the same. Our policies, procedures and activities must not discriminate, but are differentiated, as appropriate, to take account of differences of life-experience, outlook and background, and in the kinds of barrier and disadvantage which people may face, in relation to:

    ☐ disability, so that reasonable adjustments are made

    ☐ ethnicity, so that different cultural backgrounds and experiences of prejudice are recognised

    ☐ gender, so that the different needs and experiences of girls and boys, and women and men, are recognised.

    Principle 3: We foster positive attitudes and relationships, and a shared sense of cohesion and belonging
    We intend that our policies, procedures and activities should promote:

    ☐ positive attitudes towards disabled people, good relations between disabled and non-disabled people, and an absence of harassment of disabled people

    ☐ positive interaction, good relations and dialogue between groups and communities different from each other in terms of ethnicity, culture, religious affiliation, national origin or national status, and an absence of prejudice-related bullying

    ☐ mutual respect and good relations between boys and girls, women and men, and an absence of sexual harassment

    Principle 4: Staff recruitment, retention and development
    We ensure that policies and procedures should benefit all employees and potential employees, for example in recruitment and promotion, and in continuing professional development:

    ☐ whether or not they are disabled

    ☐ whatever their ethnicity, culture, religious affiliation, national origin or national status

    ☐ whichever their gender.

    Principle 5: We aim to reduce and remove inequalities and barriers that already exist
    In addition to avoiding or minimising possible negative impacts of our policies, we take opportunities to maximise positive impacts by reducing and removing inequalities and barriers that may already exist between:

    ☐ disabled and non-disabled people

☐ people of different ethnic, cultural and religious backgrounds

☐ girls and boys, women and men.

Principle 6: We consult widely

People affected by a policy or activity should be consulted and involved in the design of new policies, and in the review of existing ones. We involve:

☐ disabled people as well as non-disabled

☐ people from a range of ethnic, cultural and religious backgrounds

☐ both women and men, and girls and boys.

Principle 7: Society as a whole should benefit

We intend that our policies and activities should benefit society as a whole, both locally and nationally, by fostering greater social cohesion, and greater participation in public life of:

☐ disabled people as well as non-disabled

☐ people of a wide range of ethnic, cultural and religious backgrounds

☐ both women and men, girls and boys.

Action plans

6. We recognise that the actions resulting from a policy statement such as this are what make a difference.

7. Each year we draw up an action plan within the framework of the overall school improvement plan, setting out the specific actions and projects we shall undertake to implement the principles in paragraph 5 above..

The curriculum

8. We keep each curriculum subject or area under review in order to ensure that teaching and learning reflect the seven principles in paragraph 5 above.

Ethos and organisation

9. We ensure that the principles listed in paragraph 5 above apply to the full range of our policies and practices, including those that are concerned with:

☐ learners' progress, attainment and achievement

☐ learners' personal development, welfare and wellbeing

☐ teaching styles and strategies

☐ admissions and attendance

☐ staff recruitment, retention and professional development

☐ care, guidance and support

☐ behaviour, discipline and exclusions

☐ working in partnership with parents, carers and guardians

☐ working with the wider community.

Addressing prejudice and prejudice-related bullying

10. The school is opposed to all forms of prejudice which stand in the way of fulfilling the legal duties referred to in paragraphs 1 and 2:

☐ prejudices around disability and special educational needs

☐ prejudices around racism and xenophobia, including those that are directed towards religious groups and communities, for example antisemitism and Islamophobia, and those that are directed against Travellers, migrants, refugees and people seeking asylum

☐ prejudices reflecting sexism and homophobia.

11. There is guidance in the staff handbook on how prejudice-related incidents should be identified, assessed, recorded and dealt with.

12. We take seriously our obligation to report regularly to the local authority about the numbers, types and seriousness of prejudice-related incidents at our school and how they are dealt with.

Roles and responsibilities

13. The governing body is responsible for ensuring that the school complies with legislation, and that this policy and its related procedures and action plan are implemented.

14. A member of the governing body has a watching brief regarding the implementation of this policy.

15. The headteacher is responsible for implementing the policy; for ensuring that all staff are aware of their responsibilities and are given appropriate training and support; and for taking appropriate action in any cases of unlawful discrimination.

16. A senior member of staff has day-to-day responsibility for co-ordinating implementation of the policy.

17. All staff are expected to:

   ☐ promote an inclusive and collaborative ethos in their classroom

   ☐ deal with any prejudice-related incidents that may occur

   ☐ plan and deliver curricula and lessons that reflect the principles in paragraph 5 above

   ☐ support pupils in their class for whom English is an additional language

   ☐ keep up-to-date with equalities legislation relevant to their work.

Information and resources

18. We ensure that the content of this policy is known to all staff and governors and, as appropriate, to all pupils and their parents and carers.

19. All staff and governors have access to a selection of resources which discuss and explain concepts of equality, diversity and community cohesion in appropriate detail.

Religious observance

20. We respect the religious beliefs and practice of all staff, pupils and parents, and comply with reasonable requests relating to religious observance and practice.

Staff development and training

21. We ensure that all staff, including support and administrative staff, receive appropriate training and opportunities for professional development, both as individuals and as groups or teams.

Breaches of the policy

22. Breaches of this policy will be dealt with in the same ways that breaches of other school policies are dealt with, as determined by the headteacher and governing body.

Monitoring and evaluation

23. We collect, study and use quantitative and qualitative data relating to the implementation of this policy, and make adjustments as appropriate.

24. In particular we collect, analyse and use data in relation to achievement, broken down as appropriate according to disabilities and special educational needs; ethnicity, culture, language, religious affiliation, national origin and national status; and gender.

Date approved by the Governing Body:

Source: This model policy was developed in Derbyshire, drawing for some of its phrasing from documents developed by other local authorities and by the Department for Children, Schools and Families.

Background and acknowledgements

In its overall framework the Derbyshire model policy for belonging, difference and equality is based on the model race equality policy that it developed in response to the Race Relations Act 2000, and that was included in *Here, There and Everywhere: belonging, identity and equality in schools* published by Trentham Books for Derbyshire Advisory and Inspection Service in 2004.

The list of principles at paragraph 5 is adapted from material in *Equality Impact Assessments: a workbook*, published by the Department for Children, Schools and Families in December 2007.

The model statement takes into account guidance issued by other local authorities. These include Buckinghamshire, Cambridgeshire, Dudley, Durham, Hertfordshire, Newcastle and Sheffield.

Legal requirements

Schools are permitted by law to do any of the following:

- draw up three separate policy statements, relating to disability, ethnicity and gender respectively

- draw up a single statement containing three separate sections

- draw up a single statement containing three recurring themes or threads, as in the model Derbyshire statement.

If a school opts for the third of these, it must ensure that each of the three threads is explicitly mentioned throughout, as in the Derbyshire model.

The Derbyshire model

The Derbyshire model contains the following features.

- The term *ethnicity* is used in preference to *race* or *racial group*, on the grounds that it better reflects the intentions and concerns of race relations legislation.

- There are references where appropriate to religious affiliation and identity.

- There are references where appropriate to sexual identity and to challenging homophobia.

- The duty to promote community cohesion is integrated into the policy, particularly but not only in the third of the seven principles.

- Disability, ethnicity and gender are referred to in alphabetical order, not in the order in which legislation requiring equality schemes and policies was introduced.

Action and evaluation

Introductory notes

Guidance issued jointly by Ofsted and the Department for Children, Schools and Families states that schools should ask themselves two essential questions:

- How well are we doing?
- How can we do better?

These questions are relevant to compliance with equalities legislation as to all other aspects of a school's life and work.

This chapter sets out specific questions schools may wish to ask themselves in relation to equalities legislation. For convenience, the questions are grouped under the seven headings in Ofsted's self-evaluation form (SEF).

The questions in this chapter are not all equally relevant in every school. They are not, that is to say, a score-sheet or tick-list, to be read and considered everywhere point-by-point. Rather, they are offered as a prompts for governing bodies and senior leadership teams as they draw up action plans in the light of national legislation on belonging, difference and equality.

SEF section 1: Characteristics of the school

Ofsted's guidance on the SEF recommends that later sections of the form should be completed before the first section, particularly those which are concerned with achievement and standards, and with personal development and wellbeing. For someone reading the SEF, however, it is the opening section on the school's characteristics which sets the scene.

1. What is the composition of the school population, broken down by ethnicity, gender and year group?

2. Are we confident that the quality of this data is reliable, or could it be improved?

3. What disabilities and special educational needs do members of the current school population have?

4. Are we confident the quality of this data about disabilities is reliable, or could it be improved?

5. What is the composition of the teaching, administrative and support staff, broken down by ethnicity, gender and grade level?

6. Are we confident the quality of this data about the composition of the staff is reliable, or could it be improved?

Ofsted expects the opening section of the SEF to conclude with a list of the school's main priorities for development. Nationally, though not necessarily all in any one school, the key challenges and priorities relating to disability equality include those which are listed below.

National priorities for development: disability

- ensuring that disabled people are actively involved in the design, development, review and delivery of policies that affect them

- ensuring that a range of programmes (including work-related and work-based) is available and suitable for disabled pupils, so that they may progress and achieve

- increasing the meaningful participation of disabled people in higher and further education

- developing information, advice and guidance (IAG) for disabled people, including those with learning difficulties, so that they are fully aware of learning, career and work opportunities, and of funding and assistance available to them

- addressing low levels of awareness and understanding of disability issues amongst the general public and amongst employers, employees and providers of skills training, and in this connection promoting wider understanding of the distinction between disability and impairment and of the social model of disability.

National priorities for development: ethnicity

Nationally, though not necessarily all in any one school, the key challenges and priorities relating to ethnicity equality include:

- reducing and removing inequalities in success rates between different communities by raising the attainment and improving rates of progression in English, mathematics and science at Key Stage 2 and GCSE for certain communities, particularly those of African-Caribbean, Bangladeshi, Gypsy, Pakistani, Roma, Somali, Traveller or Turkish heritage

- improving the induction and integration and thus attainment and progression of newly-arrived pupils and in particular those for whom English is an additional language

- reducing the disproportionate number of school exclusions among African-Caribbean pupils

- addressing low take-up of childcare (including early education), especially by African, Bangladeshi, Gypsy, Pakistani, Roma and Traveller families, and the resulting impact of this on lower than average achievement by members of these communities in the Foundation Stage at age 5

- promoting community cohesion through teaching children and young people to value diversity and understand and respect others; creating a common sense of belonging; developing the skills of participation and responsible action; eliminating variations in outcomes for different communities; and providing means for children and their families to interact with people from backgrounds different from their own

- ensuring that issues of religious identity, faith, values and affiliation are taken into account in ethnicity equality policies and projects.

National priorities for development: gender
Nationally, though not necessarily all in any one school, the key challenges and priorities relating to gender equality include:

- tackling gender stereotyping and segregation in education through information, advice and guidance (IAG) in relation to subject choices and careers, and through ensuring that work experience and work-related learning give both girls and boys an opportunity to expand their horizons by trying out non-traditional work

- increasing the number of girls studying science in both academic and vocational education, thus helping to address the skills shortage in science and engineering

- In this and other ways addressing the under-representation of women in science (including computer science), engineering, construction and technology (SECT), as pupils, teachers, researchers and practitioners, and on SECT-related public bodies

- ensuring that health-focused programmes have due regard for gender differences in areas such as sexual health, mental health and obesity

- raising attainment levels in literacy for boys, in particular those who are in low socio-economic status categories

- challenging and reducing sexual harassment of girls, and the attitudes towards relationships and conflict resolution that underlie such harassment.

SEF section 2: Views of children, their parents and carers, and other stakeholders

7. What measures have we taken to consult and involve disabled people, and the parents and carers of disabled pupils, in the development of policies to promote disability equality?

8. What measures have we taken to consult and involve pupils from a range of ethnic, cultural and religious backgrounds, and their parents and carers, to promote ethnicity equality?

9. What measures have we taken to consult and involve both girls and boys, and both women and men, in the development of policies to promote gender equality?

10. What are the principal messages we have received from such consultations and involvement?

SEF section 3: Achievement and standards

11. What information do we have, broken down by both gender and ethnicity, on achievement at the end of Key Stages 1, 2, 3 and 4?

12. At what stages and in which specific school subjects are there unequal outcomes relating to ethnicity and gender?

13. What are our plans for reducing unequal outcomes?

SEF section 4: Personal development and wellbeing

14. Do we have a written code of practice which clearly outlines specific procedures to be followed for recording and dealing with prejudice-related bullying, as also with other kinds of abuse and bullying, on the school premises, and on journeys to and from school?

15. Is there shared understanding amongst staff – including support and administrative staff as well as teachers, and temporary staff as well as permanent – of ways in which prejudice-related bullying is both similar to and different from other kinds of bullying?

16. Do we train lunchtime staff and learning mentors to identify prejudice-related bullying and to follow school policy and procedures on anti-bullying?

17. Does a senior member of staff have responsibility for ensuring that incidents of prejudice-related bullying are appropriately dealt with and recorded?

18. Do we take practical steps to ensure we are aware of pupils' experiences of bullying, for example through anonymous surveys and reporting, and through focus group discussions?

19. Do pupils consider that the school has a history of taking prejudice-related incidents seriously and following them up?

20. Has a user-friendly leaflet been provided for pupils and their parents on what to do if they experience prejudice-related hostility against them?

21. Ofsted states that responses to prejudice-related bullying should be 'swift, proportionate, discreet, influential and effective'. Do pupils agree that this is how our own school operates?

22. Are pupils involved in mediating in disputes and peer mentoring, and as buddies and befrienders?

23. Are statistics on bullying at our school provided in age-appropriate language to pupils, for example at assemblies and meetings of the School Council?

24. Do parents know who to contact if they are worried about bullying?

25. Do we work with parents and other people in the local community to address tensions beyond the school gates that may be played out within school?

26. Are parents confident that any report they make to the school about bullying will be received sympathetically and supportively, and dealt with swiftly and effectively?

27. Do we provide information about sources of advice, support and assistance such as Parentline Plus?

SEF section 5: Quality of provision

Ofsted expects each of the sub-sections – teaching and learning, the curriculum, care, guidance and support – to show how the school's provision contributes to its good outcomes, or is aimed at improving weaker outcomes.

28. Do we have staff consensus on key principles and ideas that should be taught in all subjects?

29. Have we identified positive activities dealing with disability, ethnicity and gender that can be undertaken in each curriculum subject or area, and at each key stage?

30. Have we audited curriculum materials in current use, and added to them as necessary in order to ensure that they reflect the achievements and experience of women as well as men, of disabled people, and of Britain as a culturally diverse society?

31. Have we reviewed, expanded and improved our citizenship and PSHEE programmes to ensure they reflect issues in the national equalities agenda?

32. Have we given sustained attention to the concept of gender-inclusive teaching, as for example described and discussed on the Standards Site at http://www.standards.dfes.gov.uk/research/themes/gender/?

33. Do we ensure liaison with other cluster schools on curricular issues, as also across departments and areas in each school?

34. Do we make good use of positive role models, for example poets, storytellers and artists?

35. Do we have exchanges or contacts with schools in other countries or other areas of Britain?

36. Do we organise from time to time a multicultural or international day, or a 'diversity day'?

37. Do we make good use of drama, role-play, creative writing, music and art in our teaching about equalities?

SEF section 6: Leadership and management

38. Has our policy statement on equalities been thoroughly discussed by, and is it kept under review by, pupils and parents as well as by staff?

39. Do the minutes of meetings of the governing body reflect serious commitment to implementing the spirit and letter of equalities legislation?

40. Do we use data on attainment, broken down by both ethnicity and gender, to review the school's progress over time and in comparison with other schools, and to identify areas for improvement and development?

41. Do we give a high profile to rights and responsibilities by, for example, promoting the United Nations Convention on the Rights of the Child and the UNICEF programme on Rights Respecting Schools?

42. Does the general ethos of the school, as seen in displays, assemblies and curriculum materials, reflect and affirm diversity of language, culture, sexuality, religion and appearance? Does it challenge gender stereotypes? Are there positive images of disabled people?

43. Is the school involved from time to time in national projects such as *Kick Racism Out Of Football, Islamic Awareness Week, One World Week, Black History Month, Anti-Bullying Week* and *Refugee Week?*

44. Have we reviewed opportunities in the National Curriculum to teach about various kinds of intolerance and prejudice, and justice, fairness and non-discrimination?

45. Do we ensure there are references to equality and cultural diversity issues in the school's programmes and plans for induction and staff training of both teaching staff and support staff, and also for the governing body?

46. Do we consider the methods and content of staff training on race equality and cultural diversity issues, and how such training is appropriately evaluated?

47. Do the quality and robustness of our school's self-evaluation, and the way in which senior managers demonstrate that they understand and tackle improvement priorities, provide persuasive evidence that we take very seriously our responsibilities to comply with both the spirit and the letter of equalities legislation?

SEF section 7: Overall effectiveness and efficiency

Ofsted and the DCSF indicate that the final section should draw together the SEF as a whole. The section should provide a statement about the overall effectiveness of the school and should not simply provide a list of what was stated earlier. If schools' leaders and managers are clear about the progress pupils make in their learning and personal development they will find it easy to make clear links between this and the other sections. Schools might wish to set out the section as a commentary which starts by stating '*We are a good school because...*'

Legal frameworks

At present (early 2009) there are three major pieces of equality legislation affecting schools in Britain, concerned respectively with disability, ethnicity and gender. Later in the year the government will publish proposals for simplifying and streamlining the duties which schools and other public bodies have to fulfil.

This chapter summarises the duties currently in force. The requirements in them distinguish between a) 'the general duty' and b) 'specific duties'. A further distinction is drawn between a) specific duties concerned with policy development and service delivery and b) specific duties concerned with employment.

The three frameworks are described below. In addition, towards the end of the chapter, there is brief information about several other pieces of legislation.

Disability equality
The general duty
The Disability Discrimination Act 1995, as amended by the Disability Discrimination Act 2005, places a general duty on public authorities to promote disability equality. The duty came into force on 4 December 2006 and requires public authorities to:

- promote equality of opportunity between disabled persons and other persons

- eliminate unlawful discrimination

- eliminate harassment of disabled persons that is related to their disabilities

- promote positive attitudes towards disabled persons

- encourage participation by disabled persons in public life

- take steps to take account of disabled persons' disabilities, even where that involves treating disabled people more favourably.

Specific duties
The specific duties relating to policy development and service delivery require public authorities to:

- produce and publish a disability equality scheme (DES) demonstrating how they intend to fulfil their general and specific duties

- involve disabled people in the development of the scheme

- produce an action plan setting out the key actions an authority will take to promote disability equality

- explain the methods they use for assessing the impact of their policies and practices, or the likely impact of their proposed policies and practices, on equality for disabled persons

- assess and consult on the likely impact of proposed policies on the promotion of disability equality

- monitor policies for any adverse impact on the promotion of disability equality

- publish the results of these assessments, consultation and monitoring

- report annually on the progress of the action plan

- review the scheme every three years.

The specific duty covering an authority's role as an employer is to monitor the effect of its policies and practices on disabled persons, and in particular the effect on the recruitment, development and retention of disabled employees.

Ethnicity equality

In 2000, the Race Relations Act 1976 was amended to give public authorities a new statutory duty to promote race equality. On page 43 of this book there is an explanation of why for most purposes the concept of *ethnicity* is used in preference to *race* or *racial group*.

The general duty
The general duty requires public authorities to have due regard to the need to:

- eliminate unlawful racial discrimination

- promote equality of opportunity

- promote good relations between persons of different racial groups.

Specific duties

The specific duties relating to policy development and service delivery are to do with the content of a race equality scheme (RES). Schemes should set out an authority's functions and policies, or proposed policies, that are assessed as relevant to the general duty to promote ethnicity equality and should set out an authority's arrangements for:

- assessing and consulting on the likely impact of its proposed policies on the promotion of race equality

- monitoring its policies for any adverse impact on the promotion of race equality

- publishing the results of such assessments and consultation

- ensuring public access to information about the services that it provides

- training staff in connection with the general and specific duties

- reviewing the scheme every three years.

The specific duties covering an authority's role as an employer are to:

- monitor by ethnicity the numbers of staff in post and the applicants for employment, training and promotion.

- monitor by ethnicity the numbers of staff who receive training; benefit or suffer detriment as a result of performance assessment procedures; are involved in grievance procedures; are the subject of disciplinary procedures; cease employment

- report and publish annually the results of staff monitoring, and actions taken towards achievement of overall ethnicity equality objectives.

It should be noted that the specific duties for educational establishments are slightly different in their phrasing from those affecting other public bodies.

Gender equality

The general duty

The Equality Act 2006 amends the Sex Discrimination Act 1975 to place a statutory duty on all public authorities, when carrying out their functions, to have due regard to the need to:

- eliminate unlawful discrimination and harassment

- promote equality of opportunity between men and women

Specific duties

The specific duties relating to policy development and service delivery require public authorities to:

- produce and publish a gender equality scheme (GES) showing how they will meet the general and specific duties and setting out their gender equality objectives

- gather and use information on how their policies and practices affect gender equality

- assess the impact of their policies and practices, or the likely impact of their proposed policies and practices, on equality between women and men

- consult stakeholders in the development of the scheme

- assess functions and policies, or proposed policies, which are relevant to gender equality

- implement the actions set out in the scheme within three years

- report annually on the progress of the action plan

- review the scheme every three years.

The specific duties covering an authority's role as an employer are to:

- consider the need to have objectives that address the causes of any differences between the pay of men and women that are related to their sex

- gather and use information on how its policies and functions affect gender equality in the workforce.

The gender duty is intended to shift the burden from the individual having to make a complaint about unequal treatment, to the public body having to demonstrate that it is taking active steps to promote equality. The duty is also important as it highlights issues of multiple discrimination: women, men and transgender people may suffer discrimination and unequal treatment not only on the basis of their gender, but also on the basis of their ethnicity, age, disability, sexuality, and religion or belief.

At present (January 2009) requirements relating to other equality and diversity strands are not so detailed. The relevant laws and regulations are summarised briefly below.

Employment Equality (religion or belief) Regulations 2003

These regulations, which came into force in December 2003, apply to vocational training and all facets of employment, including recruitment, terms and conditions, promotions, transfers, dismissals and training. They make it unlawful on the grounds of religion or belief to discriminate directly or indirectly against anyone, subject someone to harassment, victimise someone because they have made or intend to make a complaint or allegation or intend to give evidence about a complaint of discrimination on the above grounds or to discriminate or harass someone in certain circumstances after the working relationship has ended.

Part 2 of the Equality Act 2006

Part 2 of the Equality Act 2006 makes it unlawful for providers of goods, facilities or services to discriminate on grounds of religion or belief. It also makes it unlawful for a public authority exercising a function to do any act which constitutes discrimination on these grounds. Part 2 of the Equality Act 2006 came into force in April 2007.

Employment Equality (sexual orientation) Regulations 2003

These regulations, which came into force in December 2003, apply to vocational training and all facets of employment, including recruitment, terms and conditions, promotions, transfers, dismissals and training. They make it unlawful on the grounds of sexuality to discriminate directly or indirectly against anyone; subject someone to harassment, victimise someone because they have made or intend to make a complaint or allegation or intend to give evidence to a complaint of discrimination on the above grounds or to discriminate or harass someone in certain circumstances after the working relationship has ended.

Human Rights Act 1998 and Article 14 of the European Convention on Human Rights

Article 14 refers to the prohibition of discrimination and states that the enjoyment of the rights and freedoms set forth in the Convention shall be secured without discrimination on any ground such as sex, race, colour, language, religion, political or other opinion, national or social origin, association with a national minority, property, birth or other status.

Gender Recognition Act 2004

The Gender Recognition Act 2004 (GRA, 2004) provides for the legal recognition of the transsexual person in their acquired gender and their opportunity to acquire a new 'birth' certificate for their new gender. This is called a Gender Recognition Certificate (GRC) and will replace the originating birth certificate in all official documentation. The holder of a GRC is not obliged to inform their employer that they have one, but if they choose to do so this information on their gender history must be clearly established as 'protected information'. Trans people are protected by the SDA, as amended by the Sex Discrimination (Gender Reassignment) Regulations 1999 and the Sex Discrimination (Amendment of Legislation) Regulations 2008. However, they do not need to hold a GRC.

Employment Equality (Age) Regulations 2006

From 1 October 2006, the Employment Equality (Age) Regulations make it unlawful to discriminate against workers, employees, job seekers and trainees because of their age. The regulations cover recruitment, terms and conditions, promotions, transfers, dismissals and training.

The Equality Act (Sexual Orientation) Regulations 2007

The Equality Act (Sexual Orientation) Regulations 2007, made under section 81 of the Equality Act 2006, make it unlawful for providers of goods, facilities or services to discriminate on grounds of sexual orientation. They also make it unlawful for a public authority exercising a function to do any act which constitutes discrimination on these grounds. The regulations came into force in April 2007.

Equalities in the UK: a timeline since 1918

Introductory note

The items in this list are nearly all about the development of legislation in the UK. The list also contains some references to the wider international context, and to seminal reports and iconic events. It does not aim to be exhaustive. There are three purposes: a) to show that equalities legislation has a long international history b) to show that it has been developing and that there have been many developments since 2000, and c) to recall some of the events and landmarks that can be researched by pupils. At the end, there are links to other, more detailed, lists relating to specific strands.

Before 1960

1918   On 6 February royal assent is given to the *Representation of the People Act*: women may now vote in general elections providing they are over the age of 30 who are householders or the wives of householders, or occupiers of property with an annual rent of £5, or graduates of British universities

1928   *Equal Franchise Act* is given royal assent on 2 July: women now have the vote on the same terms as men. They use it for the first time on 30 May 1929

1948   *SS Windrush* docks at Tilbury on 22 June: symbolic birthday of multi-ethnic Britain

1948   10 December, the *Universal Declaration of Human Rights* sets the global framework for equalities legislation in the decades to follow

1949   *La Deuxième Sexe* by Simone de Beauvoir, translated three years later into English: foundational text on gender equality, and on concepts of self and other

1955   *Brown v. Board of Education*, landmark case in the United States, handed down on 17 May, rules that concept of 'separate but equal' is unlawful

1957   *The Wolfenden Report* published on 7 September: turning point in official attitudes towards countering homophobia in western countries

1960s

1963   Civil Rights March on Washington and Dr King's 'I have a dream' speech, 28 August

1967   *Sexual Offences Act* receives royal assent, partially decriminalising sex between men

1969   *Colour and Citizenship: a report on British race relations* by E.J.B Rose and co-authors, foreword signed off in February: critical review of government policies

1969   On 28 June the *Stonewall Riots* in New York are the symbolic start of campaigns for full sexuality equality throughout western countries

1970s

1975   *Sex Discrimination Act*, introducing the concept of indirect discrimination into UK law and setting up a powerful enforcement agency, the Equal Opportunities Commission

1976   *Race Relations Act*, building on two acts of the previous decade: stress on avoiding indirect discrimination and setting up of a powerful enforcement agency, the Commission for Racial Equality

1978   *The Warnock Report*: foundational text on special educational needs

1980s

1985   *The Swann Report (Education for All)*, published in March: 'report of the committee of inquiry into the education of children of ethnic minority groups'

1990s

1995   *Disability Discrimination Act* addresses the discrimination that many disabled people face. Different parts of the legislation take effect at different times, and the original Act has been subject to several amendments. Key concepts include reasonable adjustment and, more recently, the social model

1995   Beijing Women's Conference is a boost to gender equality issues throughout the world

1998   *Human Rights Act 1998* and *Article 14 of the European Convention on Human Rights* state that the enjoyment of the rights and freedoms set forth in the Convention shall be secured 'without discrimination on any ground such as sex, race, colour, language, religion, political or other opinion, national or social origin, association with a national minority, property, birth or other status'

1998   *Fair Employment and Treatment (Northern Ireland) Order* making it unlawful to discriminate on grounds of religious belief and/or political opinion (later amended to include other dimensions of equality too)

1999   *Report of the Stephen Lawrence Inquiry (The Macpherson Report)*: the concept of institutional racism introduced into public consciousness and debate

1999   *Disability Rights Commission Act* sets up a powerful enforcement body

Since 2000

2000   *Race Relations (Amendment) Act*: places a positive duty on public authorities to promote race equality, and requires each to produce a race equality scheme (RES) and regular race equality impact assessments (REIAs)

2000   European directives on race and employment set the international context in which UK equalities legislation will develop through the coming decade

2000   *The Future of Multi-Ethnic Britain (The Parekh Report)* stresses three essential values: equality; recognition and respect for difference; and cohesion and a sense of shared belonging

2003   On 10 July 2003 the House of Lords votes overwhelmingly to repeal Section 28 of the Local Government Act in England and Wales

2003   *Employment Equality (Religion or Belief) Regulations* come into force on 2 December: unlawful to discriminate in employment on grounds of religious affiliation

2003   *Employment Equality (Sexual Orientation) Regulations* come into force on 1 December: unlawful to discriminate in employment on grounds of sexuality

2004   *Civil Partnership Act* receives royal assent on 18 November, giving same-sex couples the same rights and responsibilities as married heterosexual couples. It comes into operation on 5 December 2005

2005   *Disability Discrimination Act* places a positive duty on public authorities to promote disability equality, and requires each to produce a disability equality scheme (DES) and regular disability equality impact assessments (DEIAs)

2005   *Employment Equality (Age)* Regulations come into force on 1 October

2006   *Equality Act* receives royal assent on 16 February: extends religion or belief and sexual orientation regulations to cover service delivery as well as employment; places a positive duty on public authorities to promote gender equality; and requires each to produce a gender equality scheme (GES) and conduct regular gender equality impact assessments (GEIAs)

2006   *The Racial and Religious Hatred Act* receives royal assent on 16 April, amending the Public Order Act 1986, creating offences involving stirring up hatred against persons on religious grounds

2007   Public authorities increasingly combine their RES, DES and GES into a single equality scheme (SES), and their REIAs, DEIAs and GEIAs into single equality impact assessments (EQUIAs)

2007   *Equality Act (Sexual Orientation) Regulations 2007* become law on 30 April, making discrimination against lesbians and gay men in the provision of goods and services unlawful

2007   The CRE, EOC and DRC cease to exist independently and from 1 October and are brought together into the Equality and Human Rights and Commission (EHRC)

2008   In the Queen's Speech on 3 December it is confirmed a new *Equality Bill* will be published in 2009 and that a single equality duty will require public bodies 'to consider the diverse needs and requirements of their workforce, and the communities they serve'

2009   On 17 January President Obama announces wide-ranging developments and improvements in equalities legislation in the United States.

For fuller details

For *disability equality* issues, from prehistory to the 2000s, there is an extremely detailed timeline at http://www.cdp.org.uk/documents/timeline/timeline02.htm

For *ethnicity equality*, timelines include:

Developments in Britain, 1933- 2006 http://www.britkid.org/si-postwartimeline.html

Legislation in various countries: http://83.137.212.42/sitearchive/cre/downloads/timeline.pdf

With particular regard to *gender equality* events and law, 1867-2005, there is a substantial timeline at http://www.wrc.org.uk/includes/documents/cm_docs/2008/t/timeline.doc

For lesbian, gay, bi-sexual and trans equality, 1270-2007, there is a timeline at http://www.stonewall.org.uk/information_bank/history__lesbian__gay/89.asp#6

Useful websites

1. Alliance of Civilisations

Set up by the United Nations, the project aims to improve understanding and cooperative relations among nations and peoples across cultures and religions and, in the process, to help counter the forces that fuel polarisation and extremism. Masses of information on their website, in a range of world languages. Particularly worth clicking on *Media Literacy Education* and *Education about Religions and Beliefs.*
http://www.unaoc.org/content/view/63/79/lang,english/

2. Alliance for Inclusive Education

'Alfie' for short: a national campaigning network of individuals, families and groups working to help change the education system, based on their conviction that all young people need to be educated in a single mainstream education system that enables them to learn, play and live with each other. Many ideas, campaigns, resources and stories.
http://www.allfie.org.uk/index.html

3. Anne Frank House

There are several websites teaching about antisemitism and racism, and tolerance and anti-bias education more generally, through the inspiration of Anne Frank's diary. Links to most of them are accessible through the site of Anne Frank House, based in Amsterdam.
www.annefrank.org

4. Anti-Defamation League

Founded in 1913, the ADL website is frequently updated with comment on current affairs. You may wish to click first on *Education* on the home page. But note there's also a wealth of information behind *Civil Rights, Combating Hate, Extremism,* and several others.
http://www.adl.org/

5. Antisectarian Education

'Don't give it, don't take it': definitions and vivid practical suggestions for primary and secondary classrooms, with a recently added section on Islamophobia. Intended for schools across Scotland, but the approaches are relevant in many other contexts as well.
http://www.ltscotland.org.uk/antisectarian/index.asp

6. Association of Women in Science and Engineering

Aims to advance the participation of girls and women in the sciences, including biomedicine, mathematics, the social sciences, technologies and engineering, in all areas and at all levels.
www.awise.org

7. Center for Holocaust and Genocide Studies

Based at the University of Minnesota, many resources for teachers including poetry and a series of articles on '*visualising otherness*'.
http://www.chgs.umn.edu/

8. Centre for Research in Education & Gender (CREG), University of London

CREG was established to provide a networking facility for teachers and researchers concerned with gender, sexuality and anti-sexist practice in schools and colleges.
www.ioe.ac.uk/ccs/centres/creg.html

9. Centre for Studies on Inclusive Education

'A detailed consideration of the barriers experienced by some pupils can help us to develop forms of schooling that will be more effective for all pupils.' Many reports and practical resources and guidelines.
www.inclusion.uwe.ac.uk/csie

10. Citizenship Foundation

Many ideas for teaching about current affairs and controversial issues, including situations in the Middle East, and several valuable discussions and ideas about planning and organising lessons about prejudice and discrimination.
www.citizenshipfoundation.org.uk.

11. Civil Rights Movement

About 50 short articles on the history of the civil rights movement and on civil rights today, mainly in the UK, and containing many references to equality and diversity issues.
http://www.civilrightsmovement.co.uk/

12. Cohesion Bradford

Explains and explores national and local initiatives in community cohesion in schools and provides a forum for teachers and others to share experiences, views and good practice.
http://www.cohesionbradford.org/

13. Commission on British Muslims and Islamophobia

The full text of the Commission's 2004 report, plus also some extracts from it. More recently, there's the full text of *The Search for Common Ground: Muslims, non-Muslims and the UK media*, plus several articles similarly about depictions of Islam in the media.
www.insted.co.uk/islam.html

14. Convention on the Rights of Persons with Disabilities

Information on all aspect of the UN Convention, including details about the International Day celebrated each year on 3 December.
http://www.un.org/disabilities/

15. Council for Arab British Understanding

Contains resources for citizenship education, particularly in relation to media literacy.
www.caabu.org/education

16. Council for Disabled Children

Umbrella body for the disabled children's sector in England, with links to the other UK nations. Lots of information, frequently updated. Their news digest is a quarterly round-up of all the essential policy and practice news involving disabled children and young people, and their families.
http://www.ncb.org.uk/Page.asp?sve=785

17. Disability Equality in Education

'This is a human rights issue about equality in the classroom – not just an issue of special needs.' DISEED provides training consultancy, advocacy and advice; publications include the resource pack *Implementing the Disability Discrimination Act in schools and early years settings*.
http://www.diseed.org.uk/

18. East End Eye

Lively collection of resources around identity, prejudice, discrimination and equalities. Based in east London but of relevance everywhere.
http://www.eastendeye.org.uk/lgbt/

19. Educators for Social Responsibility

Based in New York, with specialist interests in conflict resolution and critical thinking.
http://www.esrmetro.org/about.html

20. Engender

An information, research and networking organisation for women in Scotland.
www.engender.org.uk

21. E-quality Women's Website

Seeks to promote an awareness of equality for women. Supports and networks with women's and other voluntary sector organisations that work for women.
www.e-quality-women.co.uk

22. Equality North West

Promotes a mainstreaming equal opportunities agenda by working with a range of partners from across the region at both strategic and operational levels.
www.equality.org.uk

23. European Commission's Women's Information Website.

The European Commission maintains this website to enhance public access to information about its initiatives and European Union policies in general.
http://europa.eu.int/comm/employment_social/ equ_opp/redirect.html

24. European Women's Lobby

Aims to eliminate all forms of discrimination against women and to serve as a link between political decision-makers and women's organisations at EU level.
www.womenlobby.org

25. Facing History and Ourselves

'By studying the historical development and the legacies of the Holocaust and other instances of collective violence, students learn to combat prejudice with compassion, indifference with ethical participation, myth and misinformation with knowledge.' The site is invaluable for teaching about antisemitism – but also other forms of racism, and about current and recent issues such as the Danish cartoons about Islam.
www.FacingHistory.com

26. Fawcett Society

National organisation, working to create greater equality for women in Britain and for change on issues at the heart of women's daily experience.
www.fawcettsociety.org.uk

27. Forum Against Islamophobia and Racism

Useful range of recent newspaper articles and several valuable factsheets. The press cuttings that come out three or four times a week are of particular interest.
http://www.fairuk.org/

28. Gay, Lesbian & Straight Education Network

American organisation working to ensure safe schools for all students, regardless of sexual orientation and gender identity.
www.glsen.org/

29. Gender Identity Research and Education Society

Promoting understanding of gender identity and variance and on challenging transphobic bullying. contains clear and authoritative information, teacher-friendly guidance on dealing with situations, and stories and quotations from young people.
http://www.gires.org.uk/transbullying.php

30. *Guardian* newspaper

There is a special section archiving all articles and reports about race equality since 1998. Also, there are links to other relevant sections, for example on British Islam, Multicultural London and the Middle East.
www.guardian.co.uk/race

31. Hometown

Set up by the Anti-Bullying Alliance (ABA), this is a lively and engaging site for children and young people about dealing with bullying, including racist bullying. Lots of conversations and stories for role-play, discussion and further research.
http://www.anti-bullyingalliance.org/walkthru.htm

32. Human Rights and Equal Opportunity Commission

The official government site in Australia dealing with anti-discrimination legislation. The section on race includes some excellent teaching materials on media treatment of refugees and immigration and these are readily transferable to UK contexts. The link takes you straight to them.
http://www.hreoc.gov.au/info_for_teachers/ face_facts03/index.htm

33. Humanities Education Centre

Includes a superb collection of webquests. Titles include *Creating a Powerful School Council, Fair Trade, Tropical Rainforests,* and *Refugees.*
http://www.locococo.org/theProject/Locococo/HE Chomepg/HECindex.htm

34. Institute of Race Relations

Many key articles and a large archive of links to news items in the local press throughout UK. Plus a weekly newsletter about current and recent events, well worth subscribing to.
www.irr.org.uk

35. Islam Awareness Week

A wealth of information and links to other sites, geared in particular to the needs and interests of teachers.
http://www.iaw.org.uk/

36. Islam Expo

Inspiring wealth of information about Islamic culture, achievements and creative developments in modern Britain.
http://www.islamexpo.com/

37. Kick It Out

The national campaign against racism in football. The website includes useful materials and practical ideas for schools, as does that of *Show Racism the Red Card* (see below).
http://www.kickitout.org/

38. Kiddiesville Football Club

'The Kiddiesville team are truly unique/with a colourful strip and a badge of mystique./The players are all different in their own special way./who respect one another and have a sense of fair play.' Very lively and enjoyable site about the exploits of an imaginary football team, with music, stories, games, humorous and nonsense verse, and vivid graphics. Also, explanatory background notes for teachers.
www.kiddiesvillefc.com

39. Kids

Support, resources and ideas for disabled young people and their families.
http://www.kids.org.uk/

40. LGBT History Month

Many practical ideas relating to school organisation and classroom teaching.
http://www.lgbthistorymonth.org.uk/

41. Lift Off Initiative

Lots of practical ideas for teaching about human rights in primary schools, developed in Northern Ireland and the Republic of Ireland.
http://www.liftoffschools.com/

42. Mencap

The leading UK charity for people with a learning disability and their families. Campaigns, publications, resources.
http://www.mencap.org.uk/

43. Morningside Center for Teaching Social Responsibility

Large number of lesson plans and ideas for classroom activities to do with current affairs. Intended for schools in the United States but containing much that is relevant and valuable elsewhere.
http://www.morningsidecenter.org

44. No Outsiders

Project in primary schools across Britain around issues of sexuality equality, which has produced books for teachers
www.nooutsiders.sunderland.ac.uk

45. Office for Disability Issues

The ODI provides information about all aspects of UK legislation on disability equality.
http://www.officefordisability.gov.uk/

46. Persona Dolls

The dolls and their stories are powerful tools for exploring, uncovering and confronting bias. They help children to express their feelings and ideas, think critically, challenge unfair treatment and develop empathy with people who are different to themselves.
www.persona-doll-training.org

47. Philosophy for Children

'We need above all to help children develop the general disposition to think better': the practical techniques and theoretical insights of Philosophy for Children (P4C) are highly relevant for teaching about controversial issues, particularly issues to do with prejudice. The website gives a flavour of the approach and information about courses and publications.
www.sapere.net

48. Press for Change

'Nowhere else in the world will you find such a comprehensive collection of information about the trans rights campaign, and details about the legal, medical, political and social issues surrounding the people it represents.'
http://www.pfc.org.uk/

49. Primary Colours

Lesson plans and resources for teachers on cultural diversity, including many on the theme of journeys.
http://www.primarycolours.net/index.php

50. Racism No Way

Based in Australia, but with much that is entirely relevant, valuable and up-to-date for teachers and pupils in other countries. Fact sheets, classroom activities, quizzes, webquests, news items, and links to recent articles from around the world.
http://www.racismnoway.com.au/

51. Reading Islam

Guidance on moral and spiritual questions for Muslims, particularly those who live in Western countries, with much of interest for non-Muslims.
http://www.readingislam.com/servlet/Satellite?pagename=Zone-English-Discover_Islam/DIEZone

52. Real Histories Directory

Set up by the Runnymede Trust (see below), a resource for teachers, parents, pupils and the wider community to support teaching and learning about cultural diversity in the UK.
http://www.realhistories.org.uk/

53. Refugee Education

Provides a regular bulletin for teachers providing information about events, courses and new publications, and acting as a forum for the exchange of news and guidance.
http://www.refugeeeducation.co.uk/index.html

54. Rethinking Schools

An online journal based in the United States, with frequent articles on race equality and racism. Some of the articles are theoretical, others are vivid and anecdotal accounts of everyday life in schools and classrooms. Use the *Search* facility to find what you want.
www.rethinkingschools.org

55. Runnymede Trust

Many articles and materials about ethnicity and race, including several dealing with education, including *Tell Me What I Need To Know*, an online resource intended for parents.
http://www.runnymedetrust.org/

56. Schools Out

Wealth of stories, case studies, information and teaching ideas relating to sexuality equality in schools.
http://www.schools-out.org.uk/

57. Show Racism the Red Card

The national campaign against racism in football, with much material of direct interest to pupils in schools. Includes information about a new DVD on Islamophobia, previewed in association with the NUT on 1 October 2008.
http://www.srtrc.org/

58. Stonewall

Online advice and information relating to sexuality and details of campaigns and policies aiming to achieve equality for lesbians, gay men and bisexual people.
http://www.stonewall.org.uk/

59. TANDIS

Short for Tolerance and Non-Discrimination Information System. Intended for policy-makers at national government level rather than for teachers but gives a sense of the overall field internationally. Scroll down to the bottom of the home page to see the range of information available.
http://tandis.odihr.pl/

60. Tide Centre

Based in Birmingham, formerly the Development Education Centre. A wealth of useful information and materials about global and international dimensions in the curriculum.
http://www.tidec.org/index.html

61. Tanenbaum

'Children don't begin life filled with fear, hatred and negative stereotypes, but attitudes form early. We train educators to prepare students to thrive in a multicultural, multi-religious society by providing training and cutting-edge multicultural curricula.' Vast collection of resources and ideas for teachers. Perhaps start by looking at their *Seven Principles,* in *Programs/Education/Our Pedagogy.*
http://www.tanenbaum.org/about.html

62. Tender

London-based organisation that promotes healthy relationships based on equality and respect. Its TRUST project aims to help young people develop positive attitudes towards relationships and to challenge anti-social and abusive behaviour. Useful resources include the Trust card game.
www.tender.org.uk

63. Teaching Tolerance

A range of lesson plans and ideas, many of them about current affairs, with a particular but not exclusive emphasis on 'race' issues.
http://www.tolerance.org/teach/index.jsp

64. Tikkun Community

Founded by people of Jewish heritage, but members include people of other faiths, plus agnostics, humanists and 'orthodox atheists'. Click first, perhaps, on 'Our Core Vision', 'The Left Hand of God' or 'The Ten Commitments' (a radical re-interpretation of the Ten Commandments).
http://www.tikkun.org/

65. Unicef

Unicef UK has been developing the concept of a Rights Respecting School and sees this as very relevant to countering all kinds of bullying in schools, including prejudice-related bullying.
http://www.unicef.org.uk/tz/teacher_support/index.asp

66. Voice Our Concern

A project in the Republic of Ireland to teach about human rights issues, including racism and xenophobia. Many practical ideas, games and activities. The involvement of prominent writers, artists and film directors is one of the project's several striking features.
http://www.voiceourconcern.org/index.htm

67. Womankind

Valuable resources, campaigns and projects addressing sexual harassment and bullying in schools
http://www.womankind.org.uk

68. Women in Science, Engineering and Technology

Information on the policies, initiatives and actions in the UK that open the doors of SET to women and help them climb the ladder to success.
www.britishcouncil.org/science/women

69. World of Difference Institute

A project of the Anti-Defamation League (see above). Classroom activities and lesson plans for anti-bias and tolerance education with the whole age-range (in American parlance, K-12), stimulating, imaginative and practical.
http://www.adl.org/education/edu_awod/ awod_classroom.asp

70. Yad Vashem

The Holocaust Martyrs' and Heroes' Remembrance Authority was established in 1953 by an act of the Israeli Knesset to be the Jewish people's memorial to the murdered Six Million and to symbolise the ongoing confrontation with the rupture engendered by the Holocaust. You may wish to click first on *The Middle East Conflict, Antisemitism and the Holocaust* or else on *Seven Poems, Seven Paintings* within the Education area.
http://www.yadvashem.org/

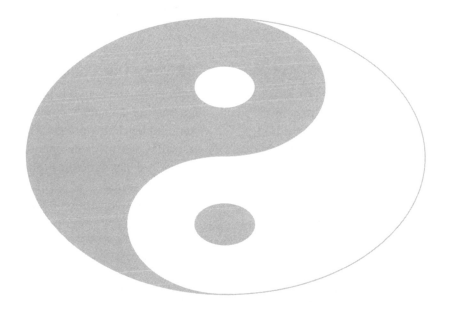

Notes and sources

Introduction (pages iii-ix)
Jay-Z: the stage name of Shawn Corey Carter (born 1969), American hip-hop artist.

Jerome Bruner: *Toward a Theory of Instruction*, outlining the objectives of *Man: a course of study* (MACOS), adapted into inclusive language, Harvard University Press, 1973.

Jim Cotter: *Prayer at Night*, Cairns Publications 1988, pp. 56-7.

Age (pages 2-3)
University of Kent research: *Equalities, Diversity and Prejudice in Britain: results from the 2005 National Survey* by Dominic Abrams and Diane Houston for the Cabinet Office Equalities Review, 2005.

See ME: the full text of the poem, known as 'Kate' or 'Crabbit Old Woman' is widely available on the internet. It was written by Phyllis McCormack, a nurse at Sunnyside Hospital, Montrose, Scotland, in the early 1960s, as explained at http://www.empowerthe spirit.com/articles/Kate.pdf.

Philip Larkin, interview with *The Observer*, reprinted in *Required Writing*, Faber and Faber 1983, p.49.

Class (pages 4-5)
Cabinet Office: *Getting On, Getting Ahead*, November 2008, followed by the Social Mobility White Paper, January 2009.

Disability (pages 8-9)
UN Convention on the Rights of Persons with Disabilities: in December 2008 it was stated in the House of Lords that the UK government expected to ratify the convention in spring 2009.

The report about attitudes towards children: 'The shame of Britain's interance of children', published by Barnardo's on 17 November 2008.

This different thinking: Secretary of State Report on Progress towards Disability Equality in the Children's and Education Sector, December 2008, p.34.

Micheline Mason: Inclusion and meaningful work, *Inclusion Now*, winter 2006/7.

Social model of disability: the term was coined in the early 1980s by Dr Mike Oliver. The tabulation on page 9 is adapted from one which appears on the website of Disability Equality in Education.

Ethnicity (pages 10-11)
Nitin Sawnhey: Trust and betrayal, in *Cultural Breakthrough: the essays*, Voluntary Service Overseas, 2004.

Racisms: based on pages 56-66 of *The Future of Multi-Ethnic Britain*, Profile Books 2000.

Martin Jacques: The global hierarchy of race, *The Guardian*, 20 September 2003.

You can't look: quoted in *Preventing and Addressing Racism in Schools* by Berenice Miles, London Borough of Ealing, 2004.

Faith (pages 12-13)
Madeleine Albright: Interreligious understanding and the battle of ideas, Tanenbaum Memorial Lecture, 4 June 2008, New York.

References to religion: Open door by Ian Mayes, *The Guardian*, 5 December 2005.

Rowan Atkinson: Every joke has a victim, *The Guardian*, 30 January 2006.

James Baldwin: Letter from a region of my mind, *The New Yorker*, 17 November 1962, republished as Down at the Cross in *The Fire Next Time*, 1963.

Bob Dylan: third track on *The Times They Are A'Changin'*, 1964.

Gender (pages 14-15)
Violence and abuse: *The Guardian*, 2 April 2008.

Sexuality (pages 16-17)
Desmond Tutu: Homophobia is as unjust as that crime against humanity, apartheid, *The Times*, 1 July 2004.

Lutz van Dijk: Introduction to *Challenging Homophobia: teaching about sexual diversity*, Trentham Books 2007.

World (pages 18-19)
Eleanor Roosevelt: launch of *In Your Hands*, United Nations Commission on Human Rights, New York, 27 March 1958

Prejudice-related bullying (pages 29-33)
Anila Baig: Multiculturalism in Britain today, has it worked?, Channel Four, April 2007.

Howard Zehr: *The Little Book of Restorative Justice*, Pennsylvania: Good Books.

Incidents for discussion: adapted from *Bullying around Racism, Culture and Religion*, Teachernet website, Department for Education and Skills 2007.

Talking and acting to learn (pages 37-41)
Bullock Report: *A Language for Life*, report of the committee of enquiry chaired by Sir Alan Bullock, 1975, paragraph 10.12

Changing language (pages 42-46)
What happened?: Duke of La Rochefoucauld-Liancourt, on the evening of 14 July 1789.

Art (pages 48-49)
The experience was liberating: Lydia Burchill (Brit School, Croydon) about her painting Appearance in *Young Brits at Art*, Royal Albert Hall, 2006, published by Commission for Racial Equality, p.51.

Will Gompertz: My life in art: the day Bourgeois moved me to tears, *The Guardian*, 8 October 2007.

Citizenship (pages 50-51)
Brian Wren: *Education for Justice*, SCM Press 1977.

Design and technology (pages 52-53)
John Eggleston: What is Design and Technology? in *A Vision for Today: John Eggleston's writings on education*, Trentham Books 2004, pp 146-7.

Patricia Murphy: Design and Technology, in *Genderwatch: still watching*, edited by Kate Myers and Hazel Taylor, Trentham Books 2007, pp. 176-7

English (pages 54-55)
P.L.Travers: The world of the hero, *Parabola* vol 1 (i), republished in *What the Bee Knows: reflections on myth, symbol and story*, Penguin Books 1994

History (pages 58-59)
Malorie Blackman: A story that must be told, *The Guardian*, 2 February 2007

Modern foreign languages (pages 64-65)
Hugh Starkey: Language teaching for democratic citizenship, in *Citizenship and Language Teaching*, edited by Audrey Osler and Hugh Starkey, Trentham Books 2005, p.36.

Kip Cates: Teaching for a better world: language education in Japan, in *Citizenship and Language Teaching*, edited by Audrey Osler and Hugh Starkey, Trentham Books 2005, p.63.

Music (pages 66-67)
Duffy: interview in *San Diego Union Tribune*, 8 October 2008.

London Undersound: review by Chris Jones, BBC, 10 October 2008.

Physical education (pages 68-69)
Albert Camus: much quoted in this form on T-shirts and posters, originating from an interview in the 1950s.

Harold Pinter: cited by Andy Bell, *The Guardian*, 27 December 2008.

Teenage years: 'Uncool' gym kit puts girls off school sport, Anushka Asthana, *The Observer*, 27 January 2008.

PSHEE (pages 70-71)
The big picture of their lives: *Challenging Violence Changing Lives: gender on the UK education agenda, findings and recommendations*, Womankind Worldwide, 2007

Religious education (pages 72-73)
Julian of Norwich: *Revelations of Divine Love*, completed in about 1393. It is said to be the first book in English written by a woman.

John Hull: The education of the religious fanatic, in *Peace or Violence: the ends of religion and education?* edited by Jeff Astley, Leslie Francis and Mandy Robbins, University of Wales Press 2007, pp 46-63.

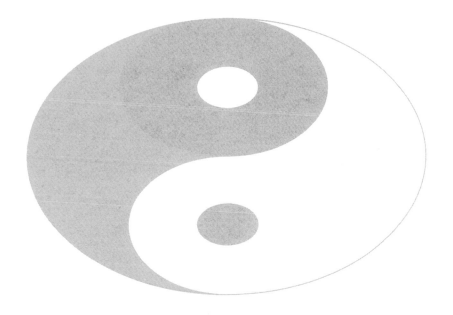